I0641130

Edward Müller

A Simplified Grammar of the Pali Language

Edward Müller

A Simplified Grammar of the Pali Language

ISBN/EAN: 9783743393295

Manufactured in Europe, USA, Canada, Australia, Japa

Cover: Foto ©Thomas Meinert / pixelio.de

Manufactured and distributed by brebook publishing software (www.brebook.com)

Edward Müller

A Simplified Grammar of the Pali Language

TRÜBNER'S COLLECTION

OF

SIMPLIFIED GRAMMARS

OF THE PRINCIPAL

ASIATIC AND EUROPEAN LANGUAGES.

EDITED BY

REINHOLD ROST, LL.D., PH.D.

XII.

PALI.

BY EDWARD MÜLLER, PH.D.

TRÜBNER'S COLLECTION OF SIMPLIFIED GRAMMARS OF THE PRINCIPAL ASIATIC AND EUROPEAN LANGUAGES.

EDITED BY REINHOLD ROST, LL.D., PH.D.

I.
HINDUSTANI, PERSIAN, AND ARABIC.
BY THE LATE E. H. PALMER, M.A.
Price 5*s*.

II.
HUNGARIAN.
BY I. SINGER.
Price 4*s*. 6*d*.

III.
BASQUE.
BY W. VAN EYS.
Price 3*s*. 6*d*.

IV.
MALAGASY.
BY G. W. PARKER.
Price 5*s*.

V.
MODERN GREEK.
BY E. M. GELDART, M.A.
Price 2*s*. 6*d*.

VI.
ROUMANIAN.
BY R. TORCEANU.
Price 5*s*.

VII.
TIBETAN.
BY H. A. JASCHKE.
Price 5*s*.

VIII.
DANISH.
BY E. C. OTTÉ.
Price 2*s*. 6*d*.

IX.
OTTOMAN TURKISH.
BY J. W. REDHOUSE.
Price 10*s*. 6*d*.

X.
SWEDISH.
BY E. C. OTTÉ.
Price 2*s*. 6*d*.

XI.
POLISH.
BY W. R. MORFILL, M.A.
Price 3*s*. 6*d*.

XII.
PALI.
BY EDWARD MÜLLER, LL.D.

Grammars of the following are in preparation :—

Albanese, Anglo-Saxon, Assyrian, Bohemian, Bulgarian, Burmese, Chinese, Cymric and Gaelic, Dutch, Egyptian, Finnish, Hebrew, Khassi, Kurdish, Malay, Russian, Sanskrit, Serbian, Siamese, Singhalese, &c., &c., &c.

LONDON TRÜBNER & CO., LUDGATE HILL.

A

SIMPLIFIED GRAMMAR

OF THE

PALI LANGUAGE.

BY

E. MÜLLER, Ph.D.

LONDON:

TRÜBNER & CO., LUDGATE HILL.

1884.

LONDON:
GILBERT AND RIVINGTON, LIMITED,
ST. JOHN'S SQUARE, CLERKENWELL ROAD.

TO

REINHOLD ROST, LL.D., PH.D.

THESE PAGES ARE INSCRIBED

AS A TOKEN OF SINCERE GRATITUDE AND FRIENDSHIP.

PREFACE.

In sending the present essay of a Pâli Grammar to the press, I feel bound to say a few words of explanation as to the plan I have followed. First of all, I must state that it was not my intention to give a complete Grammar of the Pâli Language, as this can only be done when all the principal books of the Buddhist Canon will have been published; nor was it my intention to write a Comparative Grammar of Indian vernaculars, as for this purpose the space granted to me would have been too small. I only intended to help the students of Buddhistical literature, by collecting the idiomatical peculiarities of the sacred language, comparing it chiefly to Sanskrit, and in a few cases also to the other Indian vernaculars. As the publication of Pâli texts has taken so wide dimensions during the last ten years, I thought it would not be out of place to consider and work out the new materials that have come into our possession through these books, mostly unknown to Childers and the others who made Pâli Grammar an object of their studies. Even E. Kuhn, whose "Beiträge zur Pâli Grammatik" have been of great help to me, and whose plan I followed almost throughout my book, only worked from a comparatively small number of texts, and just the oldest and most interesting, like Vinaya and Jâtaka, were all but unknown to him.

It would be rather out of place in an elementary Grammar to enter into a long discussion about the age and origin of the Pâli language. A few words on the subject will be sufficient: Kuhn, following Westergaard, holds Pâli to be the vernacular of Ujjein, the capital of Mâlava at the time when Mahinda, the son of Asoka, took the sacred Canon with him to Ceylon (Beiträge, p. 7). On the other hand, Oldenberg, rejecting that tradition, considers Pâli to be the original language of the Kâlinga country (Vinayapiṭaka, Introduction, p. liv). He compares the language of the large inscription at Khandagiri (Cunningham, Corpus Inscriptionum, i. 98), and finds only very little difference between this and the Pâli. From this he concludes that there must have been, about a hundred and fifty years before Mahinda, a frequent intercourse between Kalinga and the island; in fact, that the religion, together with its language, was brought over from there to Ceylon. I had myself formed a similar idea, independently from Oldenberg, by a careful examination of the first settlements of the Gangetic tribes in Ceylon (see my Report II. to the Government of Ceylon, reprinted Ind. Ant. IX. 9); and, recently, Mr. Nevill, in the Journal of the Ceylon Branch of the Royal Asiatic Society, has pointed out that the ancient civilized and populous district of Ceylon, the so-called Kalâwa, is not to be looked for at the south coast near Galle, as most people believe, but in the north-western district of the island, which is now almost a desert. We therefore all agree that the Aryan immigrants did not come by sea from Bengal, in which case they would have landed somewhere at the east or south coast, but that they crossed over from some port in Southern India; and, under these circumstances, it is not at all unlikely that the point from which they started may have been the kingdom of Kâlinga. To the person of Mahinda we need not attach much importance from a chronological point of view, perhaps not more than to the person of Vijaya, the first Gangetic immigrant in Ceylon according to tradition.

About the age of the Pâli language it is even more difficult to form a certain opinion than about its native country. The late R. C. Childers, in the Preface to his Dictionary, p. ix., attributed a very high antiquity to it, with especial reference to an inscription on the Sthûpa of Bharhut, which contains a quotation from Cullavagga, vi. 4. This argument, however, is not conclusive, as already P. Goldschmidt pointed out in the Journal of the Ceylon Branch of the Royal Asiatic Society for 1879. It was generally expected that we would get some help from the Ceylon inscriptions for fixing the age of the Pâli language, but unfortunately this expectation has not been fulfilled, as all those inscriptions from which we might derive an argument are not sufficiently dated. Real Pâli inscriptions have not been found in Ceylon—not more than in Cambodia. Those that approach nearest are almost identical in their language with the above mentioned Khandagiri inscription. There is, for instance, the one at Kirinde (No. 57 of my Ancient Inscriptions in Ceylon), which, for palæographical reasons, I have assigned to the first or second century A.D., about the time when, according to tradition, the doctrines of Buddhism were first reduced to writing in Pâli. The language of this inscription agrees in many points with Pâli, but it is too short, and the date is too uncertain that I could follow Goldschmidt, who felt inclined to make use of it for fixing the age of the sacred language. Neither can I agree with Kern. who holds Pâli to be an artificial language altogether. It is certain that some considerable time must have elapsed before the Pâli recension of the Canon was completed, and that through the continguity of cognate vernaculars, like the Mâgadhî, a number of words and forms found their way into Pâli which originally did not belong to it: in this way the so-called Mâgadhisms, which Kern induces to prove the artificial character of the language, are easily explained. In spite of these, Pâli conserved a certain purity during the whole middle age, and even late texts like the Dâṭhâvaṃsa and Attanagaluvaṃsa (thirteenth century), although they introduce a large number of compounds after the Saṃscritic fashion, are comparatively free from dialectic peculiarities. Not before the time when the second part of the Mahâvaṃsa was composed we find a wholesale import of Sinhalisms into the language, scarcely disguised by Pâli terminations, as, *e.g.*, mahâlâno, 'Chief Secretary,' translated back from the Sinhalese mahâlaenan.

I have only occasionally attempted in this book to distinguish between the different periods of the language. When the student will have overcome the first difficulties, he will find all the necessary information on this subject in Fausböll's Introduction to "Ten Jâtakas" and Trenckner's "Pâli Miscellany." I may say here so much, that on the whole the forms of the Sinhalese MSS. are older and more genuine, while the Burmese often replace them by more modern, more common, or more regular ones. I reserve for another occasion the interesting task to prove this by comparing a certain number of MSS., especially of grammatical texts.

Another part of the Grammar, which is totally wanting in my essay, is the Syntax; but here I hope that the classical languages, with which no doubt nearly all my readers are acquainted, will fill up the gap. Sanskrit, so to say, has no Syntax at all, but expresses all the relations in a sentence merely by compounds. This way, however, was given up at an early date by the Indian vernaculars, and a form of construction was introduced which bears a close resemblance to the Syntax of the classical languages. Under these circumstances, I have thought it best, as I had no space to give a complete Syntax to add at the end the Grammar a short Jâtaka, with an analysis that might help the student to understand the Pâli construction.

The texts I principally took my examples from are the historical books Dîpavaṃsa and first part of the Mahâvaṃsa, for which I compared the new edition published by Sumangala and Baṭuwantudâwa in 1880; besides the Vinaya, the three published volumes of the Jâtaka, the Milindapanha, and the first year's publications of the Pâli Text Society, including Anguttara Nikâya, Buddhavaṃsa and Cariyâpiṭaka. The second year's publications reached me when the book was already in the press, but I availed myself of the opportunity to mention some particularly interesting forms from Thera- and Therîgâthâ and Khuddasikkhâ. Of Fausböll's Sutta Nipâta I could use for the Grammar only the stanzas given in the foot-notes of his translation ("Sacred Books," vol. xiii): the edition of the text came into my hands when I had very nearly done.

E. MÜLLER.

CARDIFF, *June*, 1884.

CONTENTS.

	PAGE
§ 1. The Alphabet	1
§ 2. Pronunciation	2
§ 3. Vowels	4
§ 4. Change of Vowels	5
§ 5. Change of Quantity	13
§ 6. Nasal Vowels	20
§ 7. Vowels Added or Dropped	23
§ 8. Consonants	24
§ 9. General Remarks referring to Consonants of Different Classes	35
§ 10. Consonants Added or Dropped	40
§ 11. Change of Consonants at the end of a word	43
§ 12. Compound Consonants	46
§ 13. Rules on Sandhi	59
§ 14. Declension	64
§ 15. Comparison of Adjectives	85
§ 16. Pronominal Inflexion	86
§ 17. Numerals	91
§ 18. Conjugation	95
Valâhassajâtaka	128

ABBREVIATIONS.

The abbreviations are the same as in Childers' Dictionary, and besides the following new ones :—

Ang. = Anguttara Nikâya ed. Morris.
Ass. S. = Assalâyanasutta ed. Pischel.
Beitr. = Beiträge zur vergleichenden sprachforschung herausgeg. von Bezzenberger.
Bv. = Buddhavaṃsa ed. Morris.
C. = Cullavagga ed. Oldenberg.
Cariy. = Cariyâpiṭaka ed. Morris.
Dâṭh. = Dâṭhâvaṃsa ed. Cumâra Swâmi.
Dhm. = Dhâtumañjûsâ ed. Baṭuwantudâwe.
Dîp. = Dîpavaṃsa ed. Oldenberg.
Gr. = Sept Suttas Pâlis ed. Grimblot.
Hem. = Hemacandra ed. Pischel.
It. = Itivuttaka.
I. O. C. = India Office Catalogue.
K. Z. = Kuhn's Zeitschrift fûr vergleichende Sprachforschung.
M. = Mahâvagga ed. Oldenberg.
M. N. = Majjhima Nikâya.
Naigh. = Naighaṇṭuka.
P. M. = Pâli Miscellany, by Trenckner.
Pâïyal. = Pâïyalacchî ed. Bühler.
Rûp. = Das sechste Kapitel der Rûpasiddhi herausgegeben von Grüwedel.
Saddhammop. = Saddhammopâyana ed. Baṭuwantudâwe.

S. N. = Sutta Nipâta ed. Fausböll.

Samanta Pâs. or S. P. = Introduction to the Samanta Pâsâdikâ in the third vol. of Oldenberg's Vinaya.

Suttavibh. = Suttavibhanga ed. Oldenberg.

Vinaya Texts = Vols. xiii. and xvii. of Max Müller's Sacred Books.

CORRIGENDA.

P. 24, line 10 from top: *Vegha* is, as Dr. Morris tells me, a mistake for *vekha* = veshka, 'leathern strap.'

P. 25, line 3 from bottom: A verb *ussati* does not exist. The correct reading is *ñassati*.

P. 112, line 5 from top: The ending *û* belongs to the third person plural.

PÂLI GRAMMAR.

§ 1. The Alphabet.

There are three Alphabets in which Pâli manuscripts are written—the Sinhalese, the Burmese and the Kambodian. They all are derived from the Açoka Alphabet used in the ancient inscriptions of India, but represent a more current and an easier style of writing. The Devanâgarî Alphabet, which was used by Spiegel in editing his Anecdota Pâlica, is never found in Pâli manuscripts. We shall, however, for the convenience of those who have studied Saṃskṛit, in the following table give the Devânagarî letters corresponding to the Sinhalese characters. Since Fausböll's edition of the Dhammapada, published in 1855, nearly all editors of Pâli books in Europe have made use of the Roman character, as being easier to learn and less tiring to the eye. Unfortunately, a uniform way of transcription has not yet been arrived at in Pâli, any more than in Saṃskṛit; but the method followed by Fausböll and Childers is now almost generally adopted, and shall also be used in this book.

I. Vowels.

a = अ. â = आ. i = इ. î = ई. u = उ. û = ऊ.
e = ए. o = ओ.

II. Consonants.

1. *Gutturals.*—k = क. kh = ख. g = ग. gh = घ.
   ṅ = ङ.
2. *Palatals.*—c = च. ch = छ. j = ज. jh = झ.
   ñ = ञ.
3. *Cerebrals.*—ṭ = ट. ṭh = ठ. ḍ = ड. ḍh = ढ.
   ṇ = ण.
4. *Dentals.* — t = त. th = थ. d = द. dh = ध.
   n = न.
5. *Labials.* — p = प. ph = फ. b = ब. bh = भ.
   m = म.
6. *Liquids.* — y = य. r = र. l = ल. v = व.
7. *Sibilants.*—s = स. h = ह. ḷ = ळ (*Vedic*).

Besides, there is the niggahîta, corresponding to the Saṃskṛit anusvâra, and marked by a small circle in the middle of the line. It is always used at the end of words, and in the middle before a sibilant. Before another consonant the nasal of the corresponding class may be used instead.

§ 2. Pronunciation.

The Pronunciation is, on the whole, the same as in Saṃskṛit. The vowels *a*, *i*, *u* are short, the others are long : *e* and *o* are only long when they stand in an open syllable, viz., before a single consonant. When they stand before two consonants they are pronounced short, but are long *metri causâ*.

The aspirates are pronounced like the corresponding surds with the addition of an *h*. Therefore *th* does not correspond to the English *th*, but rather to the German in *Thun*, *That*. *Ch* has the same pronunciation as the simple *c* = English *ch* in child.

It is very difficult for a European to pronounce the cerebrals or linguals correctly. In India and Ceylon the natives almost constantly express our dentals by their cerebrals in words taken over from our language. It seems, therefore, that our dentals agree more with their linguals in pronunciation than with their dentals. I have, however, not been able to mark in the spoken language any difference between the pronunciation of the dentals and of the cerebrals.

The nasals are pronounced according to the class to which they belong. The guttural nasal never occurs alone, but is always followed by an explosive of its class; it sounds like English *ng* or *nk* respectively. The palatal nasal sometimes occurs doubled when an assimilation has taken place (*ññ*), and then it has the sound of the Spanish *ñ* in *doña*, or of the French *gn* in campagne. The dental nasal is exactly pronounced like *n*, and the labial like *m*.

The niggahîta, or nasal breathing at the end of the word, is pronounced in Ceylon almost with the same force as a guttural nasal = English *ng* in king. Before other consonants it is only a representative of the nasal of the corresponding class, and is pronounced accordingly.

Compound consonants are almost regularly assimilated in Pâli. We therefore do not require a table of the combinations of consonants similar to that which exists in the Devanâgarî Alphabet. The rules according to which the assimilation takes place will be given in a special chapter, and the few groups of compound consonants that still exist in Pâli will be added as an appendix to the Table of Alphabets.

The pronunciation is the same as that of the single consonants.

§ 3. Vowels.

The vowels found in Pâli are the same as in Saṃskṛit, with the exception of the ṛ and ḷ vowels, and the diphthongs *ai* and *au*.

The ṛ vowel is mostly represented in Pâli by one of the other vowels:—

(1) By *a* in *accha*=*ṛiksha*, *vijambhati*=*vijṛimbhati*, Jât. i. 12; *tasita* = tṛishita, Dâṭh. iii. 44; *maṭṭha* and *maṭṭa* = mṛishṭa, *gaha* = gṛiha, *maccu* = mṛityu.

(2) By *i* in *iṇa* = ṛiṇa, 'debt;' *kisa* = kṛiça, 'lean;' *giddha* = gṛidhra, 'greedy;' *miga* = mṛiga, 'deer;' *bhisî* = bṛisî, 'mat;' *sigâla* = çṛigâla, 'jackal.'

(3) By *u* in *usabha* = ṛishabha, 'bull;' *puthu* = pṛithu, 'broad;' *pucchati* = pṛicchati, 'to ask;' *vuṭṭhi* = vṛishṭi, 'rain.'

(4) By the consonant *r* accompanied by the vowels *i* or *u*, in *iritvija* = ṛitvij, 'brahminical priest;' *rite* = ṛite, Kacc. 126; *iru* = ṛic in *irubbeda* = ṛigveda, *rukkha* = vṛiksha, *brûheti* = bṛiṃhayati; the latter root takes also sometimes the vowel *a*, as in *abbahati*, Dh. 96, and in the participle *brahâ*.

(5) By *e* in *geha*, which is already found in Saṃskṛit.

The diphthongs *ai* and *au* of the Saṃskṛit become *e* and *o* in Pâli, that is to say, they are reduced from the second degree of vowel strengthening called vṛiddhi in Saṃskṛit to the first called guṇa; this process is called vuḍḍhi by the Pâli grammarians. Examples are *Gotama* = Gautama, *Koṇḍañña* = Kauṇḍinya, *Erâvaṇa* = Airâvana, *dveḷhaka* = dvaidhaka, *mettî* = maitrî.

These diphthongs may, however, be further reduced to the simple vowels *i* and *u*, in the same way as it is done with the original *e* and *o*. We have *mitti*=maitrî, Jât. i. 468; *issariya*= aiçvarya, *ussukka* = autsukya, Dh. 268.

The rules laid down by the grammarians concerning the use of the vuḍḍhi and of the simple vowel are very lax. Kacc., p. 214, prescribes the vuḍḍhi before a single consonant, but at p. 210 he allows the forms with the simple vowel as well, e.g., *abhidhammika, vinateyya, uḷumpika.*

There are also two instances where an *u* derived from an ṛ-vowel (see above, no. 3) becomes *o* by vuḍḍhi, viz., *pothujjanika*, 'belonging to an unconverted person,' derived from *puthujjana* = pṛithagjana and *modaṅgika*, 'one who beats the drum,' derived from *mutiṅga* = mṛidaṅga.

§ 4. Change of Vowels.

A short *a* of the Saṃskṛit is subject to different changes in Pâli. It may become:—

(1) *e* in *ettha* = atra, 'there,' according to Childers, and S. Goldschmidt's Prâkritica, pp. 21—23. Kaccâyana, p. 110, derives it from *etatha* by shortening of the syllable *eta* into *e*; but Hemacandra, i. 57, has the right explanation. Similar forms are *ubhayettha*=ubhayatra, 'on both sides,' given in the commentary, Dhp. p. 96, while the text at v. 15 has *ubhayattha*, *heṭṭhâ* and *heṭṭhato*, 'below' = adhastât; *pure*, 'before,' with its compositions *puresamana*, 'the companion who precedes a bhikkhu;' *purebhattaṃ*, 'before the morning meal;' *puretaraṃ*, Dh. 84, 135; antar in *antepura* = antaḥpura, 'harem' (*antopuraṃ*, Dh. 162, 201); *antovatthumhi*, Mah. 253; *antaravatthumhi*, Jât. i. 232; *antorukkhatâ*, Jât. i. 7; *pheggu* =

phalgu, 'empty.' In *seyyâ* = çayyâ, 'couch,' the change of *a* to *e* is effected by the following *y*, and the same has taken place in *peyyâla* = pariyâya, if the derivation given by Oldenberg, K. Z. xxv. p. 315, and Trenckner, Pâli Miscellany, p. 66, is correct.

(2) *a* becomes *i* in *tipu* = trapu, 'lead,' *kaḷimbhaka* = kaḍamba, 'point,' C. v. ii. 3; *pilâla* = palâla, 'straw,' Jât. i. 382; *timisa* = tamasa, 'darkness,' Mil. 283, and *timissâ* = tamisrâ, Jât. iii. 433; *nilicchita* = nirashṭa according to Trenckner, Pâli Misc. p. 55. A great many more examples might be adduced for this change, which is a very frequent one in Pâli.

(3) *a* becomes *u* principally through the influence of a labial, that may stand either before or after the vowel, or even at some distance from it. Examples are *sammuñjanî* and *sammujjanî*, Jât. i. 161 = sammârjanî, 'a broom;' *nibbusitattâ* = nirvasitâtmâ, Grimblot, Sept suttas Pâlis, 23; *nimujjati* = nimajj, 'to sink;' *puthujja* = pṛithagja, 'common,' Fausböll, Sutta Nipâta 171; *paṇṇuvîsati* = *pañcavîsati*, 'twenty-five,' Jât. iii. 138. There are, however, also examples of this change where there is no labial contact, e.g. *thunanti*, 'they sound,' from stan (the participle *nitthanamâna* occurs at Jât. i. 463, and *nitthananta* Jât. ii. 362); *bhrûnahu* = bhrûnahan, 'killing the embryo,' Fausb., S. N. 122; *ajjuka* = arjaka, 'the white parṇâsa;' *âgu* = âgas, 'sin;' *pajjuṇṇa* = parjanya, 'cloud;' *sajju* = sadyas, 'instantly;' *sajjulasa* = sarjarasa, 'resin,' M. vi. 7. In *usûyâ* = asûyâ, 'envy,' and in *kuñkuṭṭha* = kankushṭa, 'a sort of earth,' the change is due to the assimilation of the vowels.

(4) *a* becomes *o* in *sammosa* = sammarsha, 'confusion,' Gr. 25, Mil. 266, *anto* = antar, 'inside,' and its compositions, *tirokkha* = tiraska, 'absent,' Suttavibh. i. 185.

Saṃskṛit *â* is subject to the following changes :—

(1) It becomes *e* in *pârevata* = pârâpata, 'pigeon' (pârâpata occurs at Jât. i. 242) ; *mettika* = mâtṛika, Cariy. i. 9, 11 ; *khepeti* = kshapayati, from kshap, the causative of kshi according to Trenckner, Pâli Misc., p. 76, and Senart, Mahâvastu, p. 492 ; *theto* = sthâtṛi, Brahmajâlasutta, p. 5 ; *seḷeti* = çâḍayati, 'to fall off,' Buddhavaṃsa i. 36 (*usseḷheti*, C. i. 13, 2 = Suttavibh. i. 180, is a compound of this, and has nothing to do with *ussoḷhi*, as the translators of the passage would make out, Vinaya Texts, ii. 349). The change is effected by a *y* standing before or after the vowel in *âcera*=âcârya, 'teacher,' Khuddasikkhâ xv., comp. Hem. i. 73 ; *pâṭihera* (or *pâṭihîra*) = prâtihârya, 'a miracle ;' *nibbedheti* = nirvyâdhayati, 'to transpierce,' Mah. 143.

(2) It becomes *o* in *tumo* = tmanâ, 'self,' C. vii. 2, 3, Oldenberg K. Z. xxv. 319 ; *parovara* = parâvara, from para + avara, 'perfect,' Fausb., S. N. 59, 193 ; *doso*=doshâ, 'at night ;' *dhovati* = dhâv, 'to wash.'

(3) It becomes *û* in some compositions with the root *gâ*, 'to go,' like *addhagû*, 'a traveller ;' *pâragû*, 'one who has crossed to the other side,' probably through an intermediate *o* (see no. 2), as we have *atigo*, Dhp. v. 370 ; *pârago*, Mah. 60, 250 ; *vivarantagû*, Jât. ii. 208. The same change takes place in compositions with *jñâ*, 'to know ;' as, *viññû*, 'clever ;' *sabbaññû*, 'omniscient ;' *vadaññû* = vadanya, 'bountiful,' is clearly constructed after the false analogy of these forms, but has nothing to do with *jñâ*. *Tadaññu*, Saddhammopâyana, v. 177, is composed with *jñâ*, and is different from *tadañña* = tad + anya, occurring at v. 149 of the same poem.

Saṃskṛit *i* is subject to the following changes:—

(1) It becomes *a* in *kâkaṇikâ* = kâkiṇikâ, 'a small coin;' *paṭhavî* = pṛithivî, 'the earth;' *pokkharaṇî* = pushkariṇî, 'lotus tank;' *gharaṇî* = gṛihiṇî, 'wife,' M. viii. 1, 12; *paṭaṅga* = phaḍiṅga, 'a flying insect,' Dh. 412, Mil. 272; *sâkhalya*, 'friendship,' Childers s. v. *sakhilo*, and some futures like *icchasaṃ*, *pamâdassaṃ*, mentioned by Trenckner, Pâli Misc., p. 75. A doubtful form is *ânañja*, Jât. i. 415, ii. 325; Suttavibh. i. 4; Sâmaññaphalasutta ed. Grimblot, p. 143. A various reading is *ânañca*, which is found besides in Mahâparinibbânas., p. 34, and Burnouf, Lotus, pp. 306, 467, 866; but Buddhaghosa, at Suttavibh. i. 267, explains it by *ânejjappatte*, *acale*, *niccale* and if this is correct it can have nothing to do with Saṃskṛit ânantya, but must be derived from the Pâli root *iñj* = Saṃskṛit *iṅg*, 'to move.' Comp. Childers, s. v. *ânejjaṃ*, and p. 454, and Senart, Mahâvastu, p. 399.

(2) It becomes *e* in *etta*, 'so much' = Skt. iyant, Senart, Mahâvastu, p. 384 (but not *etto*, 'hence,' which is derived from *etta* = eta, Goldschmidt, Prâcritica, p. 21—23); *vihesâ* = vihiṃsâ, 'vexation,' and the verb *viheseti*, 'to annoy,' Jât. iii. 295; *vehâgamana* = vihâgamana, 'coming through the air,' Mah. 157; *vematika* = vimatika, 'inconsistent;' *vemajjha* = vimadhya, 'the middle;' *Vessabhû* = Viçvabhû, 'a name of Buddha;' *mañjeṭṭha* = mañjishṭha, 'light red;' *keraṭika*, Jât. i. 461, and *kerâṭiya*, Jât. iii. 260 = kirâṭa, 'hypocrite,' (comp. Indian Antiquary, vi. 40); *esikâ* = ishîkâ, 'pillar' (but *isikâ*, Sâmaññaph. S. ed. Gr. p. 144), Brahmaj. S 18, neuter pl. *esikâni*, Jât. ii. 95; *terovassika*, 'more than a year old' = Skt. tirovarshika, like Vedic tiro ahnya, Morris' Report on Pâli Literature, p. 6; *dvebhâga*, *dvebhâva*, *dvebhûmaka* = dvibhâga, dvibhâva, dvibhûmaka; *pettâpiya* = pitṛivya,

Trenckner, Pâli Misc. 62; *mâtâpettibhara*, 'supporting one's parents,' = mâtṛi + pitṛibhara, *tekiccha*, 'curable,' from cikitsâ, *eṭṭhi* = ishṭi, 'wish,' Khuddasikkhâ. A difficult form is the adverb *seyyathâ*, 'just as,' in a comparison, which is explained in different ways by the grammarians. Trenckner, Pâli Misc. p. 75, explains it as a Magadhizing form, corresponding to the Skt. tadyathâ, and he is followed by Senart, Mahâvastu, p. 415, who adduces the corresponding form of the northern Buddhists sayyathidam, already mentioned by Léon Feer, Etudes Bouddhiques, p. 313. I believe this explanation preferable to that of E. Kuhn, who considers it as a potential âtmanepadam of the root *as* 'to be.' A form *seyathâ* occurs in the inscription of Bhabra, Cunningham, Corpus Inscriptionum Indicarum, p. 111. A similar change of *a* to *e* is in *yebhuyya* = yad + bhûyas, Instr. *yebhuyyena*, 'generally,' 'mostly.' The corresponding form of the northern Buddhists is yobhûyena, Senart, Mahâvastu 422.

(3) It becomes *u* in *kukkusa* = kiknasa, C. x. 27, 4, *kukku* = kishku, 'measure of length,' M. vii. 1, 5; *nicchubhîyati* = kshiv, 'to spit out,' Mil. 188; also written *nichubhati*, Cariyâp. ix. 23, Bv. xi. 15, Jât. iii. 512, 513; participle, *nicchuddha*, Mil. 130, Dh. 8, 202; *râjula* = râjila, 'a lizard;' *geruka* = gairika, 'red chalk,' M. i. 25, 15.

(4) It becomes *o* in *onojeti*, 'to dedicate,' M. i. 22, 18 = avanejayati according to Kern, Buddhism, p. 92.

Saṃskṛit *i* is subject to the following changes:—

(1) It becomes *a* in *kosajja*, 'idleness' = kausîdya; *bhasma* = bhîshma, 'dreadful,' C. vii. 4, 8 (another form *bhesma* occurs Ab. 167, and *bhisma* in the Mahâsamaya ap. Grimblot, p. 288).

(2) It becomes *â* in *tiracchâna* = tiraççîna, 'an animal.'

(3) It becomes *e* in *khela* = krîḍâ, 'play,' Dâṭh. i. 41, Pischel Beitr. iii. 254; *kelâyatha*, Mil. 73, *âvelâ* = âpîḍa, 'a garland;' Prâk. *âmela*, Hem. i. 105; *ereti*, 'to utter,' Dh. v. 134; according to Trenckner, Pâli Misc. p. 76 = *îreti*. *E* for *î* is found frequently in derivative syllables, as in the absolutive *gahetvâ* for gṛihîtvâ, in *âjâneyya* for *âjânîya*, and similar forms given by Kacc. p. 196. There is a present *seyyasi* = çîryasi, from çar, 'to throw down,' occurring only in this form Jât. i. 174, Dh. 147. The commentary explains it by *visiṇṇaphalo hoti*. Çrî becomes *se* in the names of two plants, *sepaṇṇî* = çrîparṇî and *sephâlikâ* = çrîphâlikâ.

(4) It becomes *u* in the root *ṭhubh* = shṭhîv, 'to spit;' also written *ṭhuh*, as in *niṭṭhuhati*, S. i. 132; nuṭṭhuhati, C. vi. 20, 2, M. viii. 1, 11. The form *niṭṭhuh* occurs also in Prâkṛit, Deçînâmamâlâ, iv. 41.

Saṃskṛit *u* is subject to the following changes:—

(1) It becomes *a* in *sakkhali* = çashkuli, Jât. ii. 281, Suttavibh. i. 55; *agaru* and *agalu*=aguru, 'Agallochum;' *dudrabhi* = dundubhi, 'drum,' M. i. 6, 8; *vâkarâ* or *vâkara*, Jât. iii. 541 = vâgurâ, 'net;' *phallati* = phull, 'to bear fruit,' and *pharati* = sphur, 'to flash.' *Bâhusacca* is derived by Childers from bâhuçrutya, by Fausböll from bâhusmârtya; the analogy of *muṭṭhasacca*, however, adduced by Childers, points to the latter etymology. *Rathesabha*, 'king,' is according to Trenckner, Pâli Misc. p. 59 = ratheçubh; according to Senart, Mahâvastu, p. 427 = ratha + ṛishabha.

(2) It becomes *i* in *dindima* = dundubhi, 'drum,' Dîp. 96; *khipati* = kshu, 'to sneeze;' *muditâ* = mudutâ, Senart, Mahâvastu 629. The identity of *sippî* and çuktî, 'pearl oyster,' assumed by Trenckner, Pâli Misc. 60-75, remains doubtful.

(3) It becomes *o* chiefly before a double consonant, as in *okkâ* = ulkâ, 'torch,' Jât. i. 34; *pottha* = pusta, 'a modelled figure,' Jât. ii. 432, and its derivative, *potthalikâ* or *potthanikâ*, M. vi. 23, 3, C. vii. 3, 4; Prâk. *puttaliâ*, Pâïyalacchî 117; *vokkamati* = vyutkramati (comp. Pischel's remarks to Hem. i. 116); *pâmokkha*=pramukhya (*pâmukkha*, Jât. i. 371). There are, however, also instances of the change before a single consonant, as *kolañña* = kulaja, 'of good family,' Mil. 256 (for the termination comp. *aggañña* and Senart's remarks Mahâvastu, p. 617); *koliya*, Jât. iii. 22, and *kolîniya*, Jât. ii. 348 (if the reading *koleyya* is not to be preferred, *kulîna* occurs at Mah. 245); and *kolaputti*, which is not to be considered as a *vuḍḍhi* with Trenckner, Pâli Misc. p. 64. Pâli *koṭi* represents the Skt. kuṭi as well as koṭi, Lotus 432; *anopama*, Jât. i. 89; Mahâvastu 511 is = *anupama*, Mah. 240.

Saṃskṛit *û* is subject to the following changes:

(1) It becomes *â* in *masâraka* = masûraka, 'a sort of bed,' C. vi. 2, 3. *Bhâkuṭi*, Suttavibh. i. 181=bhrûkuṭi, 'eye-brow,' most probably goes back to the Skt. bhrakuṭi or bhṛikuṭi. The common Pâli word *bhamu* is not, as Childers explained it, a careless pronunciation of bhrû, but an abbreviation of *bhamuka* or *bhamuha* = bhrûmukha, as is shown by the Prâk. bhamayâ, Hem. ii. 167. The Sinhalese baema also goes back to this form.

(2) It becomes *î* or *i* in *bhîyo*, *bhiyyo* = bhûyas, and in *niyura* = nûpura, 'bracelet,' which, however, might stand for *nidhura*.

(3) It becomes *o* in *oja* = ûrjas, 'strength,' Jât. i. 68, Dh. 132; *onavîsativasso* = ûnav°, 'less than twenty years old.'

Saṃskṛit *e* is subject to the following changes:—

(1) It becomes *a* in *milakkha* = mleccha (comp. K. Z. xxv. 327), and in some verbal forms like *akaramhasa*, Dh. p. 147.

(2) It becomes *â* in *kâyûra* = keyûra, 'bracelet,' C. v. 2, 1, Jât. iii. 437.

(3) It becomes *i* before double consonants, as in *pasibbaka* = prasevaka, 'bag'; *paṭivissaka* = prativeçaka, 'neighbouring;' *ubbilla* = udvela in *ubbillabhâva*, 'lengthiness,' Saddhammopâyana 136; but also before single ones, as *abhijîhana* from jeh, Jât. 546, v. 49, according to Trenckner, Pâli Misc. 78; *apavîṇati*, Jât. 409, v. 4, from *veṇ*; *pahiṇaka* and *paheṇaka*, 'offering,' Prâk. paheṇaya, Pâïyal. 206.

(4) It becomes *o* in *maṅkato* = matkṛite, Mil. 384; and in *atippago* = atiprage, 'too early,' corresponding to atiprâgaḥ of the northern Buddhists, Mahâvastu 418.

Saṃskṛit *o* is subject to the following changes:—

It becomes *u* before a double consonant, and *û* before a single, as in *juṇhâ* = jyotsnâ, 'a moon-lit night;' *tutta* = tottra, 'a pike used to guide an elephant,' Cariy. iii. 5, 2; *tadûpiya*, 'suitable, corresponding,' which is not = *tadrûpya*, as Childers suggested. Trenckner, Pâli Misc. p. 77, identifies it with Skt. tadopya, which is derived from the root vap in composition with *â*, and ascribes the change of *o* to *û* to the following *i*; but Senart, Inscriptions de Piyadasi i. 188, and Mahâvastu 493, takes it as a compound of tad + opaya. *Visûka* = viçoka, 'spectacle;' *dûbha* = droha, 'deceiving,' Mah. 49; *khajjûpanaka*, Trenckner, Pâli Misc. 59, for *khajjopanaka* = khadyota, 'the fire-fly;' *ârûgya* = ârogya, 'good health,' M. N. 66. Also an *o* contracted from ava is subject to this change, as in *ussâva* = avaçyâya, 'dew;' *ujjhâ* = avadhyâ, 'to blame;' and *uḍḍeti* = *oḍḍeti* = ava + ḍî, according to Morris, Anguttaranikâya i. 24, 4. Comp. the remarks of Fausböll, Two Jâtakas 13, the verb *niḍḍâyati*, Jât. i. 215, *niḍḍâpeti*, C. vii. 1, 2, identified by Oldenberg with nirdâtâ, Manu vii. 110. An example of an *o* changed to *u* before a single consonant is *ukkusa* = utkroça, 'the osprey,' only written *ukkûsa* at Jât. 486, v. 2, where the *û* is required by the metre.

§. 5. Change of Quantity.

Long vowels before a double consonant are generally shortened. The reason is given by Kacc. vii. 5, 13-14, where he says that a short vowel before a double consonant as a long vowel is called *garu*. This rule, however, is not always followed by the manuscripts, where we often find a long vowel before a double consonant, especially when the long vowel is the result of a contraction. Fausböll, in the preface to his edition of the Dhammapada, p. vii., was the first to call attention to this inconsistency of the manuscripts, and afterwards Senart, Kacc. pp. 4, 5, has discussed it at some length. The principles established by him have been followed on the whole by the recent editors of Pâli texts, as far as the groups with assimilated consonants are concerned; and also Childers, in his Pâli Dictionary, has adopted them with a few exceptions, so he writes *ŭjjavaṃ* instead of *âjavaṃ*, Kacc. 216 = Skt. ârjava, *dâbbî* = Skt. dârvî, *dâtta* = dâtra, following Abhidhânappadîpikâ. Kuhn, in his Pâli Grammar, p. 18, condemns this way of writing, and allows the long vowel only in those instances in which a contraction has taken place, as in nâgghati = na + agghati, piyâppiya = piya + appiya. The Sinhalese editions generally follow the method of the manuscripts.

Before a nasal we generally find the law observed, as *santa*, *danta*, *vanta* = çânta, dânta, vânta, Kacc. 295, but the editors of the second part of the Mahâvaṃsa write *lâṅganakicca*, Mah. 39, 28. Before other groups of consonants the editions are less consistent: we have *ativâkya*, Ab. 122, Dh. 57; *sakya*, *sakka*, *sakiya* = çâkya, Mah. 9, 55, Abh. 5, 336; *âkhyâta* and *akkhâta*, Kacc. 5, 220; *pahatvâna* = *pahâtvâ*, 'having left behind,' Dh. v. 243, 415; *dussîlya*, Dh. v. 162 = dauḥçîlya, 'wickedness;' *balya*, 'childhood,' Dh. v. 63, but *bâlya*, Ab. 250, 1079; *ñatvâ* and *bhitvâ*, from jñâ and bhî, Kacc. 303, Dh. 85, 379; *kamyatâ* = kâmyatâ, 'desire;' *bahya* = bâhya, 'external.'

Another possibility of avoiding the contact of a long vowel with a double consonant is to put the single consonant of the group resulting by assimilation, as in *âjava* = ârjava, Kacc. 216, Ten Jât. 98; *kâsu* = karshû, 'hole,' *ûmi* = ûrmi, 'wave,' Ab. 662; but *ummi*, Mil. 346; *bhâṇaka* = bhâṇḍaka, 'jar,' Suttavibh. 90, Ascoli Kritische Studien, p. 211; *bhûja* = bhûrja, 'the birch;' *ahâsi* = ahârshît,' 'he took.' The same process may take place after a short vowel, which then is lengthened, as in *sâjîva* for sajjîva = sad + jîva, 'rule of conduct,' Pât. 5, 65, comp. Senart, Mahâvastu 481; *vûpakâsati* = vyupakarsh, 'to make clear,' M. i. 25, 20, Pât. 109; *svâtana* = çvastana, 'belonging to to-morrow,' Dh. 231; *vâka* = valka, 'bark of a tree;' *saṅkâpayati* = saṅkappayati, 'to arrange,' M. iii. 1, 2 (there are, however, two various readings, *saṅkâyati*, C. x. 18, and Anguttaranikâya, p. 117, and *sankâmeti*, Suttavibh. i. 50, which render the etymology doubtful). Several compounds with the preposition *ud*, as *ûhadeti* = ud + had, 'to befoul with excrement;' *ûhata* = ud + hata, 'destroyed,' Dh. 375, Mahâvastu, 379, 566; *ûhasana*, from *ud* + *has*, 'laughter,'

Mil. 127. *Uhanati*, M. i. 49, 4, Suttavibh. ii. 40, seems to be synonymous with *ûhadati*, mentioned before; and I believe the translation given by Davids and Oldenberg, 'threw their bedding out,' not to be correct. The passive *ûhañña* is found M. i. 25, 15, the past participle *ûhata*, C. viii. 10, 3; and another compound of the same root, *ohaneti*, occurs in the same signification, Cariy. ii. 5, 4, where it is in parallel to *uccâra-passâvaṃ katvâ*, Jât. ii. 385.

The opposite way is to shorten the vowel before a double consonant, as in the instances given above, and this can also be done where a single consonant follows a long vowel. Frequent instances occur in the genitive plural of stems ending in *u* or *as;* as *bahunnaṃ* = bahûnâm, Dhp. 81, *pitunnaṃ* = pitṛîṇâm; and of numerals, as *tiṇṇaṃ*, *pañcannaṃ*. But there are also a number of other words belonging to this category; as *bhummi* = bhûmi, 'earth,' C. xii. 2, 5; *mattiṣambhava* = mâtṛis°, Dh. v. 396; *mâtumattika* = mâtṛimâtṛika, Suttavibh. i. 16; *uṇhissa* = ushṇîsha, 'diadem,' Bv. p. 68, note; *vanibbaka* = vanîpaka (which is found Cariy. i. 4, 5), 'beggar,' with change of *p* to *bb; niḍḍha* = nîḍa, 'nest,' from ni + sad, (comp. Hem. i. 106, Weber Indische Streifen i. 141, Ascoli 284); *sutta* = syûta, 'sewn;' *daṭṭha* = *dâṭhâ*, 'jaw,' Mil. 150; *abbahati* = â + bṛih, 'to take down,' and its causative *abbâheti*, 'to pluck,' M. vi. 20, 2, C. vii. 4, 5; *jaṇṇu* = jânu, 'knee,' Mahâparinibb. 69; *avassayiṃ* for *avâsayiṃ* (comm. *vâsaṃ kappesiṃ*), 'I lived,' Jât. ii. 80. Syllables ending with *y* are especially often treated in this way; as *abhibhuyya* = abhibhûya, Dh. v. 328; *bhiyyo* = *bhîyo* for bhûyas, mentioned above; *jiyyati* = jîyati, 'to decay,' Dh. 179, and the suffix *iyya* = îya.

The same transformations we have hitherto mentioned can

also take place in syllables which contain an *e* or an *o*, with the only difference that these diphthongs always remain as they are; they are considered long before a single consonant and short before a group, as stated by the grammarian Moggallâna (Alwis, Introduction, p. xvii. note, Catal. 41, 184). Generally, however, the syllable conforms to the condition, according with the etymology of a word. The following are exceptions, where the simple consonant stands for the double: *veṭheti* = veshṭayati, 'to surround;' *sekha* = çaiksha, 'a disciple;' *apekhâ* and *apekkhâ*, 'desire,' = apekshâ, *upekhâ* and *upekkhâ*, 'equanimity;' *vimokha* = vimoksha, 'release.' *Y* is always doubled after *e*, as in *seyyo* = çreyas, 'better;' *maccudheyya* = mṛityudheya, 'death:' the only exception is *keyûra*, 'bracelet,' Ab. 287, which generally becomes *kâyûra* (see above). *V* after *o* is only doubled in *yobbana* = yauvana, 'youth.' After the prefix *o*, contracted from ava, a double consonant formed by assimilation always remains, as in *abbocchinna* = avyavacchinna, 'unbroken,' Mil. 72; *okkhitta* = avakshipta, 'cast down,' Pât. 20, 21; and even a simple consonant is often doubled, as in *ossajjati* = avasṛij, 'to give up;' *ossakkamâna* = avasarpamâna, 'scattered,' Jât. i. 139; *abbhokkiraṇa* = abhyavakiraṇa, 'covering,' and, with change of *o* to *u*, *abbhukkirati*. Jât. ii. 311.

The cases of change of quantity are by no means yet exhausted by the rules and examples given above. We have numerous instances where the change is due entirely to the metre, and others again where no reason is visible. We will try in the sequel to keep separate as much as possible these two cases, and mention those instances which are supported by the Prâkṛit dialects.

The roots terminating in *â*, as *jñâ*, *dâ*, *sthâ*, almost regularly shorten the vowel in composition, and in derived forms, as, e.g., *paññavâ* = prajñâvant, 'wise,' always written with *ă* except in a passage of the Cûlakammavibhangasutta, quoted by Gogerly, Ev. 31. From sthâ we have *paṭṭhăpeti*, 'to bring forward.' The same occurs in *saṃkhata* = saṃkhyâta, Dh. v. 70, where, however, it might also be shortened by a confusion with *saṃkhata* = saṃskṛita. *Â* in the middle of a root is shortened in *gahati* and *gaheti*, 'to dive,' = gâh, and its compositions *ogahi*, Mah. 152; *ogaha*, Jât. iii. 289; *vigayhati* and *vigahâpeti*. Suffixes with long vowels are very often shortened, as, e.g., *âgahita*=âgṛihîta, 'seized,' Dh. 107; *appatita* = apratîta, 'displeased,' Pât. 4, 5; *sadevika* = sadevîka, 'accompanied by his queen,' Mah. 205; *vipaccanika* = vipratyanîka, 'hostile,' Grimblot 1; *paccanika*, Cariy. ii. 8, 4; *ahirika*=ahrîka, 'shameless,' Dh. 44; *sâluka* = çâlûka, 'the root of the water-lily,' M. vi. 35, 6. Especially the suffix *îya* is almost regularly shortened, as in *pâniya* = pânîya, 'water,' M. i. 26, 4; *sakiya* = svakîya, 'own;' *upâdâniya* = upâdânîya, 'sensual,' in a passage of the Saṃyuttaka Nikâya quoted by Oldenberg, Buddha 435; *pâṭidesaniya* = pratideçanîya, 'a class of priestly sins requiring confession,' constantly written so in the Pâtimokkha and Suttavibhanga; *gariya* = garîyas, 'heavier,' Dh. 245, &c. Shortening by svarabhakti is very frequent in Pâli, as in *bhariyâ* = bhâryâ, 'wife;' *âcariya* = âcârya, 'teacher;' *suriya* = sûrya, 'sun,' and numerous other examples.

Lengthening of vowels occurs principally, in prepositions, as in *âbhidosika*, 'stale,' from *abhidosa*, 'evening,' Suttavibh. i. 15; *pâṭibhoga* = pratibhoga, 'surety,' comp. Mahâvastu 582; *pâvacana* = pravacana, 'the Holy Scriptures' (the same in the language of the northern Buddhists, Mahâvastu 566); *pâkaṭa* = prakaṭa, 'clear, evident;' *pâheti*, 'to send' = prahi, from the false analogy of the aorist *pâhesi*; *pâyâti* and *pâyâto*, from prayâ, 'to depart,' Jât. i. 146; Rhys Davids, Buddhist Suttas, p. 241, note. There are, however, some other instances of lengthened vowels besides: *a* privativum is lengthened in *âyasakya*, 'disgraceful,' from a + yaças, Jât. ii. 33, iii. 514, in *paccâmitta* = pratyamitra, 'enemy.' Other vowels in *âlinda* = alinda, 'terrace;' *âjira* = ajira, 'court,' Mah. 215; *pâyâsa* = pâyasa, 'rice porridge;' *gâvuta* = gavyûti, 'a measure of length;' *ummâra* = udumbara, 'threshold;' *sabbâvâ* = sarvavat, 'entire;' *kharâpiṇḍa*, 'lump of glass,' Dîp. 102. Lengthening is very frequent also when a word is repeated in composition; as *phalâphala* = phala + phala, 'wild fruits, berries;' *divâdivassa*, 'at an unusual hour,' Ten Jât. 16, Ch. Addenda; *khaṇḍâkhaṇḍaṃ*, 'in pieces;' *kiccâkiccâni*, 'all sorts of duties.'

According to the law given by Kaccâyana, vii. 5, 13, that a short vowel before a double consonant is considered as a long one, we have to treat here also those cases where a single consonant after a short vowel is doubled, and a double one simplified, because the quantity of the syllable is changed by this process. In these cases it is sometimes very difficult to distinguish what is due to the metre, and what not. A clear instance of metrical change would be *appabodhati*, Dh. v. 143, if Subhûti's opinion is right, that it stands for *apabodhati*; Weber, however, and Max Müller refer it to alpabodhati, 'parvi facere,' and Fausböll to a + prabodhati. Subhûti's view is supported by *apparâjita* = aparâjita, 'unconquered,' Cariy. i. 2, 2. Other instances are *saparijjana*, 'with his attendants,' Cariy. ii. 8, 2; *kappilâyaṃ*, Cariy. ii. 9, 2; *nikkhani* for nikhani, 'he buried,' Cariy. iii. 14, 4; *abhinivassatha*, 'he lived,' Cariy. i. 10, 3; *upavassatha*, ib. i. 10, 5; *paddhâna*, Bv. xvii. 16; *uttassati* = uttrasati, 'he trembles,' Cariy. iii. 13, 4 (participle *uttrassa*, M. x. 2, 16); *suppatha*, Ab. 193; *kummiga* = kumṛiga, Mil. 346; *paggharati*, 'to ooze,' Dh. 81; *abhisammayo*, Bv. vi. 3; *paribbasâna* = parivasâna, 'abiding,' Fausböll, S. N. 152. The following are instances from prose texts where the doubling cannot be ascribed to metrical influence: *patikkûla* = pratikûla, 'contrary;' *jâtassara* = jâtasara, 'a natural pond;' *sakkâya*=svakâya, 'individuality;' *anuddayâ*=anudayâ, 'compassion and *anuddayatâ*, Suttavibh. i. 247; *vibbheda*=vibheda, 'division,' Jât. i. 212; *ummâ*=umâ, 'flax,' Mil. 118; *cheppâ*= çepa, 'tail,' M. v. 9, 1; *cikkhalla*=cikhalya, 'mud,' M. vii. 1, 1; *niggahîta* = nigṛihîta, 'restrained,' *okkassa* = avakṛishya, 'having dragged away,' Mahâparinibb. 3; *upakkilesa* = upakleça, 'sin;' *upassaṭṭha* = upasṛishṭa, 'oppressed,' Jât. i. 61; *vikkhâyitaka* from vi + khâd, comp. Kern, Buddhism, 402; *pâṭiekka* = pratyeka, 'individual' (regular form *pacceka*); *kallahâra* = kahlâra, 'the white water-lily;' *mukkhara* = mukhara, 'noisy,' Minayeff, Pât. 59; *vissajjeti*, from vi + sṛij, 'to give away,' and *avissajjiya*, *avissajjika*, C. vi. 15, 2, M. viii. 27, 5 (but *visajja* in a metrical passage Mahâparinibb. 17), and *avissaṭṭhaka*, Jât. i. 434.

Compared with these instances of doubling a consonant, the instances of the opposite process are but few, and they are nearly all to be ascribed to metrical influence. So we have *dukha* instead of *dukkha*=duḥkha, 'sorrow,' Dh. v. 83; *puṭha* instead of *puṭṭha*=pushṭa, 'fed,' Dh. v. 218; *kaṇikâ*=karṇikâ, 'an ear ornament,' Ab. 574. In prose texts I have only found *kaṇikâra* = karṇikâra, 'the tree Pterospernum acerifolium,' Jât. ii. 25; and *bhadanta*, also written *bhaddanta*=bhadrânta, 'a venerable man, a Buddhist priest.'

§ 6. Nasal Vowels.

The anusvâra or *niggahîta* can stand before every consonant, but before an explosive sound it may also migrate into the nasal of the corresponding class. So you may write *kuṃkuma* or *kuñkuma*, *saṃcarati* or *sañcarati*, *saṃḍâsa* or *saṇḍâsa*, *taṃdita* or *tandita*, *kaṃbala* or *kambala*. In the first instance, however, before a guttural it is usual to transcribe the nasal by a simple *n* without any diacritical sign. Before *h* the anusvâra can be changed into the palatal or cerebral nasal, as *pañha* = praçna, 'question,' but *paṇhi* = pṛiçni, 'variegated;' in both instances the origin of the group is the same, viz., from *çn*, but the usage has been fixed in different ways. From *pañha* is derived *apaṇṇaka* for *apaṇhaka*, 'certain,' always spelt with the cerebral group. *Paripaṇhati* is spelt with the cerebral in Minayeff's Pâtimokkha, p. 17, 92; but in the corresponding passage of the Suttavibh. ii. 141, we have *paripañhati*, which I consider to be more correct. Prâk. paṇha, Hem. ii. 75. In the same way we have *taṇhâ*=tṛishṇâ, 'thirst,' *saṇha*=çlakshṇa; but its derivative, spelt *sañhita*, Mah. 104. *Osaṇhati*, at C. v. 2, 3, is also spelt with the cerebral, and I believe this to be the correct spelling, as the *ṇ* is already found in Saṃskṛit. I cannot account for the change of *ñ* to *ṇ* in *apaṇṇattika*=aprajñaptika, 'not existing,' in *âṇâ*=âjñâ, 'order,' *âṇâpeti*, *âṇâpana*, &c.

Before a *y* the anusvâra can remain, or the whole group can migrate into *ññ*, as e.g. *saṃyoga* or *saññoga*. Before *r*, *s*, *v* it is always retained. Before *l* the anusvâra is always assimilated, as in *sallâpa* = saṃlâpa, 'conversation.' Before a vowel it becomes *m* in poetry when a short syllable is required, the nasal vowels being invariably considered as long.

The grammarian Vanaratana, according to Trenckner, Pâli Misc. 80, remarks that *h* may be joined to any one of the five nasals; for *h* with the guttural nasal I can adduce no example, but for *h* with the dental nasal we have *cinha* = cihna, 'mark,' *pubbanha*, Mil. 17; *majjhanha* = madhyâhna, 'midday,' Ab. 767; *sâyaṇha* = sâyâhna, 'evening,' seems to be always spelt with the cerebral.

The nasal vowel is sometimes replaced by a long one, as in *sîha* = siṃha, 'a lion;' *vîsati* = viṃsati, 'twenty;' *saṇḍâsa* = saṃdaṃça, 'tongs;' *dâṭhâ* = daṃshṭrâ, 'jaw.' This happens often in the preposition saṃ when it is followed by *r*, as in *sârâga* = saṃrâga, 'passion;' *sârambha* = saṃrambha, 'clamour;' *sârambhî*, 'clamorous,' Jât. iii. 259; *sârâṇîyo*, Mahâparin. 2, is according to Senart's explanation, Mahâvastu, p. 599 = saṃrañjñîya for saṃrañjanîya, and = sârâyanîya of the northern Buddhists, which etymology is confirmed by the passage of the Lalitavistara, p. 530, where we read sammodanîḥ saṃrañjanîḥ kathâḥ kṛitvâ, corresponding to the Pâli *sammodanîyaṃ kathaṃ sârâṇîyaṃ vîtisâretvâ*, comp. also Vinaya texts, ii. 364. Sârdhaṃ loses its anusvâra in the compound *saddhivihârika*, 'fellow priest,' and also in the simple word in a passage of Buddhaghosa quoted C. 318.

The opposite process is the development of an unorganic anusvâra out of an explosive consonant. This process has taken very large dimensions in the Sinhalese down from the 10th or 11th century (see my Contributions to Sinhalese Grammar, pp. 12, 13), but we find the beginning of it already in Pâli, and it is not merely the corrupt spelling of the Simhalese writers as Childers believed (see Childers, s. v. nagaraṃ). Moreover, a form nangaram occurs in the Saṃskṛit of the northern Buddhists, Mahâvastu pp. 83, 440, so that we have no reason to doubt its correctness in Pâli. *Nânga* for nâga, 'snake,' Dh. 102, occurs again in the introduction to the Samanta pâsâdikâ, and seems to be also a correct form. Other instances are *sanantana*=sanâtana, 'perpetual,' which Childers explains as sanaṃ+tana; *piñja*=piccha, 'wing,' (*piccha* occurs at M. v. 2, 3); *mahiṃsa*=mahisha, 'buffalo,' Cariy. ii. 5, 1, and *mahiṃsakamaṇḍala*, 'the Andhra country;' the insertion is especially frequent in syllables which originally contain an *r*; *sammuñjanî*=sammârjanî, 'a broom' (also written *sammujjanî*, Jât. i. 161); *saṃvarî*=çarvarî, 'the night;' *dandha*=dṛiḍha, 'slow' according to Trenckner, Pâli Misc. p. 65, and its derivatives *dandhati*, Jât. i. 345, Feer Etudes Bouddhiques 133, Cariy. viii. 13 (*dantayi* is a mistake); *dandhâyanâ*, Mil. 59, 105; *dandhayitattaṃ*, Mil. 115; *maṅkato*=matkṛite, Mil. 384; *maṅkulâ*=matkuṇa, 'bug,' Pât. 91, comp. Skt. maṅkhuna; *añc*= arc, 'to worship' according to Weber (we find, however, *accayissaṃ*, Dâṭh. v. 17, and *accita*, Ab. 750); another *añc* occurs, Jât. i. 417, to explain *udañcanî*; *sanda*=sâdra, 'thick, coarse;' *siṅgâla*=çṛigâla, 'jackal;' *vitaṃsâ*=vitastâ, Mil. 114; *nantaka* =naktaka or laktaka, 'dirty cloth,' Jât. iii. 22, which Trenckner, Pâli Misc. 81, believes to be borrowed from an aboriginal language: the regular form *lattaka* occurs Dhp. 190. Some participles must be mentioned here of verbs that have *n* in the present, as *randha*=raddha, from *randheti*, 'to destroy,' Mil. 107, Jât. 537 v. 108, 538 v. 85; *bandha*=baddha, 'bound,' Kacc. 130, M. viii. 12, 1, where Buddhaghosa has *baddhaṃ*; *pilandha*=pinaddha, from *pilandhati*, 'to rear,' Mil. 337. The aorist *agañchi*, and the future *gañchati* or *gañchîti*, from gacchati, 'to go,' occur according to Trenckner, Pâli Misc. pp. 71—74, only in Sinhalese manuscripts, while the Burmese almost constantly write *agacchi*; besides, in the compound *adhigacchati* the aorist does not take the nasal, and in the plural before *-iṃsa*, *-ittha*, *-imha*, the form *gañchi* is very rarely used. I believe these forms to have followed the false analogy of *adañchi* from *daṃç*, 'to bite,' Jât. 444 v. 3, and of *âhañchi*, M. i. 6, 8, *hañchema*, Jât. ii. 418, from *han*, 'to strike,' which both have the nasal in the root.

We often find a nasal added at the end of a word, as in *sakkaccaṃ* = satkṛitya, 'respectfully;' *kudâcanaṃ* = kudâ + cana, 'ever;' *aññadatthuṃ*=anyad+astu, 'only, exclusively;' in a passage of the Saṃyuttaka Nikâya, quoted by Trenckner, P. M. 67, *tatthañca*=tatra ca, Mah. 5. In two instances we find *n* instead of the anusvâra: *cirann âyati*, Kacc. 26, and *satânan esa dhamma* for *satânaṃ*, Jayaddisa Jâtaka. Besides, at the end of the first part of compounds, not only in such cases where it is to be considered as an accusative, as in *atalamphassa*=atalasparça, 'not touching the bottom;' *sabbañjaha*, 'leaving everything;' such instances are *viralañjana* = virala+jana, 'thinly peopled,' Att. 204; *andhantama*=andha +tamas, 'thick darkness;' *attantapa*, 'self-tormenting,' Childers s.v. *puggala*; *gaṇaṃgaṇa*, 'with many linings, M. v. 1, 30; *rathandhuri* = ratha+dḥur, 'the yoke of the carriage,' Saddhammopâyana v. 468; *kabaliṃkâra*=*kabalîkâra* (the writing of the Burmese MSS.) 'material food,' Gr. 43; *jayampatî*, 'husband and wife,' most probably standing for jâyâpati and also *tudampati*, would go back to the same form if Childers' etymology is right; comp. Kuhn's Lit. Bl., no. 1, art. 2. The contracted form *jampatî* occurs Dâṭh. iv. 25.

§ 7. Vowels Added or Dropped.

A vowel in the middle of a word has been elided in *agga* for *agra*=agâra, 'house,' only used in compounds; *dhîtâ*=duhitâ, 'daughter;' *jaggati* for jâgarati, 'to watch;' and in the termination *mhe* for mahe, of the 1st person pl., âtmanepadam.

A vowel at the beginning is dropped in *laṅkâra*=alaṅkâra, 'ornament, decoration,' Dîp. 47; *numati*=anumati, 'consent,' Dîp. 35; *valañjeti*=avalañjeti, 'to use, to spend' (the full form occurs Jât. i. 111, Suttavibh. ii. 266); *pinâsa*, 'catarrh' =*apinâsa*, Skt. pînasa; *parajjhati* for *aparajjhati*, from râdh, 'to be injured;' *pavana*=upavana, 'side of a mountain,' according to Subhûti, Jât. i. 28, and perhaps *vegha*=avekshâ, 'care,' Mahâparin. 25, Rhys David's Buddhist Suttas p. 37.

About *pi* for api, *ti* for iti, *va* for iva and eva, we shall speak hereafter in the chapter on Sandhi.

The only instance of a vowel added in the beginning of a word is *itthî*=strî (istrî in the Gâthâs of the northern Buddhists), an evolution which bears the closest similarity to that in the Romance languages, as, e.g. *ispirito*=spiritus.

§ 8. Consonants.

(1) *Gutturals.*—A Sanskrit guttural is represented by a palatal in *cunda*=kunda, 'turner,' Mil. 331; *iñj* and its compound *sammiñj* were also believed to come under this rule by Fausböll, Dhp. 273, and Weber, Ind. Stud. iii. 147, Ind. Streifen i. 131, iii. 397, who identified it with Skt. *iṅg*; other etymologies of these difficult words have been suggested since, of which I will only mention two, that of Senart, Mahâvastu p. 418, who believes *sammiñj* to stand for saṃvriñj, and that of Oldenberg, K. Z. xxv. 324, who derives it from añc. Against Senart there is only this to say, that the root vṛiñj occurs in

the form *viññ*, Suttavibh. ii. 264, in the form *viñj*, Suttavibh. i. 127 (comp. Trenckner, P. M. 59); and Oldenberg leaves the double *m* entirely unexplained. The form samiñjayati occurs also in the Bṛihad Âraṇyaka Upanishad, 6, 4, 23; and perhaps after all this may be the right etymology (Boehtlingk-Roth. s. v. sam+iṅg).

(2) *Palatals.*—A Skt. palatal is represented by a guttural in *bhisakka* = bhishaj, 'physician' (but *Satabhisaja* = çatabhishaj, Ab. 60); *milakkha* = mleccha for milaska, K. Z. xxv. 327; *pabhaṅguna*=prabhañjana, 'destruction.' Of much greater importance than this is the change of palatals to dentals, very frequent not only in Pâli but throughout the Indian vernaculars. Especially the Sinhalese, down from the 9th century, is fond of this change, of which I have given numerous examples in my Contributions to Sinhalese Grammar, pp. 17, 18. An instance of this change in Skt. is saṃsṛidbhis, from saṃsṛij, T.B. i. 8, 1, 1, Çat. B. v. 4, 5. 3. As in Sinhalese throughout, so we find in Pâli already a limited number of instances where *j* passes into *d*, and *c* to *s*, seldom into *t*: *digucchati* and *jigucchati*=jugupsati, 'to despise;' *tudampatî* compared with *jayampatî* and *jampatî*, Dâṭh. iv. 25, see Childers s. v.; *digacchâ* and *jighacchâ*=jighatsâ, 'hunger,' Pischel Beitr. iii. 249; *pariccadi* from *pariccajati*=parityaj, 'to forsake.' So *s* for *c* or *ch* in *ussita*=ucchṛita, 'lofty,' Dîp. 19, Suttavibh. i. 79 (*ucchita*, Ab. 708), and its compound *samussita* in a passage of Papañca Sûdanî Alwis. Intr. 79; another *samussita*=samuccita, 'accumulated,' occurs at Dh. v. 147; *ussaya*, Suttavibh. ii. 224, must mean 'dispute, quarrel,' but I am not sure about its etymology; *ussati*, various reading, Ang. i. 5, 5, is explained by Morris as being the present of *ussita*=ucchṛita, but I doubt very much the correctness of this identification; *ussa*=ucca,

'distinguished,' Fausböll, S. N. 164: *t* for *c* in *tikicchâ* = cikitsâ, 'medicine;' *uttiṭṭha* for *ucchiṭṭha*=ud+çishṭa, 'left over,' M. i. 24, 1, Mil. 213, 214, see also Vinaya texts i. 152; *vitacchikâ* = vicarcikâ, 'scabies.' In *upacikâ*, 'white ant'= Skt. upadîkâ, the Pâli seems to have retained the original palatal, while the Skt. has turned it into the dental: see Trenckner, P. M. 62. In *kasiṇa*=kṛitsna, 'entire,' and *dosina* =jyautsna, 'clear, spotless,' I believe the *t* to be dropped first, and then the consonants to have been separated by svarabhakti (see above, and Ascoli, Krit. Stud. 249).

(3) *Cerebrals.*—As in all Indian vernaculars cerebralization has been carried in Pâli much further than in Sanskṛit, although not so far as in Sinhalese and some other Prâkṛits. The opposite process, viz. change of a Skt. cerebral to a dental in Pâli is very rare: *cetaka*=ceṭaka, 'servant,' Suttavibh. ii. 66, Cariy. ii. 4, 7; *kotthuka*=kroshṭâ, 'jackal,' Mil. 23, 118 (*koṭṭhuka*, Jât. ii. 108); *deṇḍima*=ḍiṇḍima, 'drum,' Jât. i. 355; *dindima*, Dîp. 86, Bv. i. 32, may either be the same or=dundubhi, 'kettle-drum;' *dindibha* = ṭiṭṭibha, 'name of a bird,' Ab. 643; *kubbâna*=kurvâṇa, 'doing.' In *khânu*=sthâṇu, 'the stump of a tree,' I believe the spelling with the dental to be the correct one, as we have it Dh. 107, Mil. 34, and in *khânuka*, Jât. i. 483; as for *khaṇati*, which Trenckner, Pâli Misc. 58, 59, believes to have influenced *khânu*, it is also spelt with the dental in several instances, and where it is spelt with the cerebral this can be easily accounted for by assuming a confusion with the root, 'kshaṇ.' *Ghâna*=ghrâṇa, 'the nose,' is always spelt with the dental; *goṇa*, 'bullock,' spelt *gona*, Jât. ii. 300, is derived from the root gur, 'to growl;' *gonaka* most probably =gauṇika, 'a woollen coverlet,' Gr. 9, M. v. 10, 4 (comp. Pischel, Beitr. iii. 236). Besides, we have the dental instead of

the cerebral in the terminations of the aorist—*ittho*=ishṭhâs, -*ittha*=ishṭa.

The Pâli has one sound belonging to the cerebral class which does not exist in classical Saṃskṛit, but only in the dialect of the Vedas, viz. the cerebral *ḷ*, distinguished from the dental by a dot under the line. It is very difficult to give exact rules for the use of this *ḷ* as the manuscripts are even less consistent in this respect than with regard to the dental and cerebral *n*. Generally speaking, *ḷ* or *ḷh* between two vowels represents *ḍ*, *ḍh*, but we find it used promiscuously also for the dentals. I have collected a number of instances from Pâli texts which will illustrate the use of these sounds: *âlulati* Pât. xvi., but *âluḷati* Jât. i. 25, ii. 9, *âloḷâpeti* Alw. i. 103; *bubbula*=budbuda, 'a bubble,' Jât. i. 68, *bubbulaka*, Samanta Pâsâd. 336, but *bubbuḷa*, Mah. 175, 213, Att. 10, 190, *bubbuḷaka*, Dh. 31, 336; *palâsa*, 'leaf,' Dh. 42, but *paḷâsa*, 'pride,' Mil. 289; *kabala*, 'mouthful,' Pât. 22, Mah. 121, but *kabaḷa*, Jât. i. 68, Mil. 180, *kabaḷikâ*, M. vi. 14, 5; *kukkula*, 'hot ashes,' Ab. 36, but *kukkuḷa*, Jât. i. 73, 423; *mâla*, 'pavilion,' M. iii. 5, 9, but *mâḷa*, Gr. 2, Mil. 16, 47; *cola*, 'cloth,' Pât. 86, Mah. 219, *colaka*, C. v. 9, 4, but *coḷa*, Mil. 74, *coḷaka*, M. i. 25, 15, Mil. 53; *celukkhepa*, 'waving a cloth,' Mah. 99, 113, but *ceḷukkhepa*, Samanta Pâsâd. 336; *gâlha*, 'deep,' Jât. ii. 75, but *gâḷha*, Jât. i. 155, *gâḷhaka*, Jât. i. 265; *gâdha* also is found in a later text, Saddhammopâyana, v. 394.

(4) *Dentals.*—The change of a dental to a cerebral is generally caused by a preceding *r* in the original form of the word; for instance, *pajjuṇṇa*=parjanya, Mah. 129 (*pajjunna*, Jât. i. 331), 'cloud,' *kaṭâkaṭa*=kṛitâkṛita, 'done and undone,' M. vi. 14, 7, but *katâkata*, Dh. v. 50; *sakkaṭa*=saṃskṛita, 'Saṃskrit,' in a passage of Buddhaghosa quoted C. 322 but

sakkata, Kacc. 10; *pâsaṇḍa*, 'heretical,' most probably = pârshadya, Kern, Açoka, 58. In a great many instances, however, an *r* has no effect on a following dental, as in *muddikâ* = mṛidhvika, M. vi. 35, 6; in *attha* = artha, 'cause,' also spelt *aṭṭha* and *aṭṭa*; in the verb *vattati*, 'to begin,' = vartate (*vaṭṭati* means 'to be right,' see Childers, s. v.); *pati* and *paṭi*= prati (see Childers, s. v.); *sithila*, 'loose,' and *saṭhila*, 'crafty,' both from çrath (comp. Hem. i. 89), *sâthalika*, Ang. ii. 5, 3. The *n* of the preposition *ni* preceded by *pa*=pra is always changed into *ṇ*, as, e.g., *paṇidahati*=pranidhâ; after *pari* it is generally changed, as in *pariṇâyaka*, Mil. 38, Jât. ii. 393; we find, however, also *parinâyaka*, Mah. 63, Mahâparin. 5, and *parinaya*= pariṇaya, 'marriage,' Ab. 318, *parinibbâna*, *pariniṭṭhanti*, S. P. 332. On the other hand we have also instances where the change of a dental into a cerebral is not due to a preceding *r*, as in *sûṇâ*=çûnâ, 'a slaughter-house,' also spelt *sûnâ*, M. vi. 10, 2, Suttavibh. i. 59; *jaṇṇu* = jânu, 'knee,' Mahâparin. 69, Ab. 742; *sakuṇa*=çakuna, 'a bird;' *sakkuṇâti* =çaknoti, 'to be able;' *saṇim*, *saṇikam*=çanais, 'slowly' or 'quickly;' *sobhaṇa* = çobhana, 'resplendent;' *diṇṇa*, past participle of *dâ*, 'to give,' in *pariyâdiṇṇa*, Mil. 289; *kaviṭṭha* and *kapiṭṭha*, Jât. i. 237,=*kapittha*, 'the tree Feronia Elephantum;' *kapiṭhana*=kapîtana, 'the tree Thespesia Populneoides,' Suttavibh. ii. 35; *patisallâṇa* = pratisaṃlayana, 'seclusion,' spelt with the dental, Dîp. 63, Jât. ii. 77 and Mil. 138, v. l.; *patisallîṇa*=pratisaṃlîna, 'secluded,' spelt with the dental, M. ii. 1, 2; *vipâṭeti* = vipâteti, 'to crush,' C. v. 11, 1, if the reading introduced by Oldenberg is correct, but perhaps we ought to stick to *vipphâdetvâ*, given by the manuscripts, and derive this form from visphur with change of *r* to *d*, as in some other instances given below, p. 33. *Vibhîṭaka*=vibhîtaka, 'beleric myrobalan,' Ab. 567, Jât. ii. 161, spelt with the dental, M. vi. 6, Att. 213; *vidaḍḍhatâ*=vidagdhatâ, 'gallantry,' Att. 199; *uṇṇata*=unnata, 'high,' Ab. 289, *uṇṇametave*, Fausb. S. N. xi., *uṇṇati*, ib. 158; *saṇati*=svan, 'to sound,' Mil. 414, but *sanita*, Ab. 747, *sanantâ*, Fausb. S. N. 131. In some cases the change of the dental to the cerebral is due to the influence of a sibilant, as in most derivatives of the root sthâ, 'to stand,' e.g., *ṭhâmo*=sthâman or sthâmas, 'strength,' Gr. 121, v. l., Kacc. 315, Sutta Nipâta, 34, ap. Senart, Mahâvastu, 628, spelt also *thâmo* several times (comp. Hem. iv. 267), *ṭhâna*=sthâna, 'standing,' *ṭhapeti*, caus., &c.; exceptions are *indapatta*=indraprastha, 'name of a town;' *majjhatta*=madhyastha, 'impartial,' where the aspiration is dropped besides, and *santhâgâra*=saṃsthâ + agâra, 'a royal rest-house,' M. vi. 31, 1, Mahâparin. 60. In derivations of the root *vas*, 'to dwell,' we find the cerebral and the dental used promiscuously. The past part. is *vuṭṭha* or *uṭṭha*, Kacc. 291; in composition *adhivattha*, Jât. i. 99, *adhivuttha*, Mahâpar. 23, *upavuṭṭha*, Cariy. ii. 3, 2, *parivuṭṭha*, Pât. 6: for the absolutive *parivaṭṭhabba* in the same line we should adopt the reading given in the foot-note. The roots *dah* 'to burn,' and *das* 'to bite,' take the cerebral *ḍ* in those forms where there is no cerebral in the second syllable; there are, however, exceptions to this, as *dayheyya*, Mil. 84, Att. 192, 208, Dâṭh. iii. 10, *upadaṃseti*, Suttavibh. ii. 309; in some compositions of *dah* the *d* is changed to *ḷ*, as in *viḷayhase* (v. l. *vilayhase* and *vidayhase*), Jât. ii. 220, *âḷâhana*, 'a cemetery,' *pariḷâha*, 'fever, pain.'

D is often changed to *l*, as in *âlimpana*, 'light'=*âdîpana*, Mil. 43; *âlimpâpeti*, 'to kindle,' Suttavibh. i. 85; *dohala*=dauhṛida, 'the longing of a pregnant woman,' and *dohaliṇî*, Jât. ii. 395, Kacc. 203, *bila*=*viḍa*, 'part, bit;' in *bilasâ*, Kacc. 91, *bilaso*,

Kh. 30, *ulu*=uḍu, 'lunar mansion,' *âvelâ*=âpîḍa, Prâk. âmela, Hem. i. 105, 202, 234; *kovilâra*=kovidâra, 'Bauhinia variegata;' *uḷâra*=udâra, 'noble.' *Dh* passes into *l* in *gharagolikâ*=gṛihagodhikâ, 'lizard.' *N* is changed to *ḷ* in *ela* = enas, 'fault,' *nela*, 'faultless,' from the same, not as Trenckner suggests, from nariya (Childers, add. s. v.): comp. *anelaka*, Senart, Mahâvastu 572, *pilandhati* = pinah, 'to wear,' *piḷandhitvâ*, Jât. i. 100.

Change of *d* to *y*, forming an analogy to the ya-çruti of the Jainaprâkṛit, occurs in *goyâna*=godâna, in *Aparagoyâna*, 'name of one of the four Mahâdîpas, *sâyati*, 'to taste,'=svâdate, *khâyita*=khâdita, 'eaten,' and *kâyitabba*, C. v. 34, *vikkhâyitaka*, 'one of the Asubhakammaṭṭhânas,' Kern, Buddhism, 402. *Avâhayi*, Jât. ii. 354, must be derived from the root *had*, which we have in *ohadâmase* of the following verse.

I here add those cases where *ṭ* is changed to *ḷ* and *t* to *r* without being able to decide whether we have to adopt an intermediate form with *ḍ*, *d* or not: *âḷavî*=âṭavi, 'name of a city in India;' *âḷavika*=âṭavika, 'dwelling in forests;' *kakkhaḷa* =kakkhaṭa, 'hard, solid,' Prâk. kakkhaḍa, Pischel, Beitr. iii. 251 (*kakkaṭa*, Mah. 57); *kheḷa*=kheṭa, 'saliva,' in *kheḷâpaka*, C. vii. 3, 1=kheṭâtmaka according to Kern, Buddhism, 180; *kulaṅka*=kuṭaṅka, 'roof,' in *kulaṅkapâdaka*, C. vi. 3, 4 (v. l. *kulunkap°*); *paḷaccara*=paṭaccara, 'old clothes.'

(5) *Labials.*—*P* is changed to *m* in *sumanta*= supanta, 'sleeping,' Mil. 368; *dhûmâyati* = dhûpâyati, 'to fumigate,' Jât. i. 360, Samanta Pâsâd. 315, Dîp. 83. *Bh* is changed to *m* in *dindima*=dundubhi, 'a drum;' *m* is changed to *v* in *vîmaṃs* =mîmâṃs, Kacc. 243.

(6) Half-vowels:—

(a) *Y* is often changed to *v*, as in *kîva*=kiyant, 'how

much;' *tivaṅgika*=tryaṅgika, 'having three angas,' Saddhammop. v. 65; *tivaṅgula*=tryaṅgula, 'triangular,' Samanta Pâsâd. 336; *kaṇḍuvati* = kaṇḍûyati, 'to scratch,' Suttavibh. i. 117; *migava*=mṛigayâ, 'hunting,' M. x. 2, 15; *navutta*=nayuta, 'a large number,' Dh. 143; *sampavaṅka*=samparyaṅka, 'friend,' Mahâparinibb. 6, Feer, Etudes Bouddh. 51, Weber, Indische Streifen, iii. 397; *paṭiviṃsa* or *paṭivisa*, M. vii. 11, 1, C. xii. 1, 1, Suttavibh. i. 60=pratyaṃça, 'portion,' with samprasâraṇa, *vivina*=vijana, 'lonely,' Cariy. i. 1, 3; *pavecchati*, 'to give,' Jât. i. 28, Mil. 375, is identified with some hesitation to payacchati by Trenckner, Pâli Misc. 61. *Y* is changed to *b* in *pubba* = pûya, 'pus, matter;' *jalâbu* = jarâyu, 'the womb;' *nibbujjhati*=niryudh, 'to struggle,' C. i. 13, 2, Suttavibh. i. 180, partic. *nibbuddha*, Gr. 9, Mil. 232; to *bh* in *sarabhû*= sarayu, 'name of a river.'

Y is changed to *r* in *kuḷira*=kuḷiya, 'mattress,' according to Buddhaghosa, Suttavibh. ii. 40, 357, Pât. 86, spelt *kulîra*, C. vi. 2, 3; *vedhavera* = vaidhaveya, 'the son of a widow;' *sâmaṇera*=çrâmaṇeya, 'a novice,' Kacc. 188; *bâhira*=bâhya, 'external' (*bâhiya*, Jât. i. 422); *antarârati*=antarâyati, 'to run into danger.' It is changed to *l* in *laṭṭhi* = yashṭi, 'stick,' *jotalati* = jyotayati, 'to lighten,' Kacc. 234, *upakkamâlati* = upakramâyati, 'to manœuvre,' ib. 235; to *h* in *nahuta*=nayuta, 'a vast number,' *ranañjaha*=rañañjaya, 'victorious in the battle,' Mil. 21, Trenckner, Pâli Misc. 83, *sahampati*=svayampati, 'epithet of Brahmâ,' M. i. 5, 5, Vinaya Texts, i. 86, *upaṭṭhâhaka*=upaṭṭhâyaka, C. i. 18, 5. *Y* is changed to *j* (as in Prâkṛit, see E. M. Beiträge zur Gramm. d. Jainaprâk. p. 31) in *jantâghara*, *jantaggha*=yantragṛiha, 'bath-room,' Oldenberg K. Z. xxv. 325.

(b) *V* is changed to *y* in *dâya*=dâva, 'forest' *dâyapâla*, M.

x. 4, 2, comp. Senart, Mahâvastu, 633, *lâyati*, 'to reap,' Jât. i. 215, and *lâyeti*, Suttavibh. i. 64 = *lâveti*, *châya* = çâva, 'the young of an animal,' Ten Jât. iii. (generally *châpa*), *caccara* = catvara, 'a courtyard,' through an intermediate catyara. *V* is changed to *b* in *paribbasâna*, 'abiding,' from vas, Fausb. S. N. xii. 152; *vârabâṇa* = vâravâṇa, 'a woman's jacket;' *sibbana*, 'sewing,' = sîvana, and *sibbinî*, 'a needle,' M. viii. 1, 18, comp. Prâk. sivvinî, Pischel Beitr. iii. 260 (most probably from false analogy of *sibbati* = sîvyate, 'to sew'); *subbaco* = suvacas, 'compliant;' *subbuṭṭhi* = suvṛishṭi, 'abundance of rain;' *thabaka* = stavaka, 'a cluster of blossoms;' *balibadda* = balivarda, 'an ox;' *sambâhati* = saṃvâh, 'to shampoo,' Jât. i. 293, Suttavibh. i. 83; *sâribâ* = çârivâ, 'name of a plant;' *kabala* = kavala, 'mouthful;' *kabaḷikâ* = kavalikâ, 'compress,' M. vi. 14, 5.

V is hardened to *p* in *lâpa* = lâva, 'quail,' Jât. ii. 59; *pajâpatî* = prajâvatî, 'wife;' *pettâpiya* = pitṛivya, 'cousin,' Trenckner, Pâli Misc. 62; *palâpa* = palâva, 'chaff;' *châpa* = çâva, 'the young of an animal;' *opilâpeti*, 'to sink,' M. iv. 1, 3, vi. 26, 6, according to Trenckner, Pâli Misc. 63, from plu (Childers, add. derives it from pîḍ); *avâpurati*, 'to open' *apâpuṇanti amatassa, dvâraṃ*, It. 84, v. 2, and *pâpurati* or *pârupati*, 'to dress,' from var; *apadâna* = avadâna, 'legend;' and also *sapadânaṃ*, 'regularly,' (Trenckner, Mil. 428, derives it from sapadi + ayana, which I do not quite understand) = sa + avadâna, according to Senart, Mahâvastu, 595; *supâṇa* = suvâna, 'dog,' Mil. 147; *dhopana* = dhovana, 'cleaning,' Jât. ii. 117; *sipâṭikâ* = çivâṭikâ, M. vi. 7. C. v. 11, 2, 27, 3 (in the two latter passages, however, it seems to have another meaning—Buddhaghosa explains it by *kosaka*, 'a sheath').

(7) Liquids:—

The change of *r* to *l* is frequent enough in Pâli, although not quite so frequent as in some other Indian dialects, especially the Mâgadhî of the inscriptions. Instances are *ludda*=rudra, 'dreadful,' Trenckner, Pâli Misc. 59; *lujjati*=ruj, 'to break,' M. viii. 21, 1 (Dhm. vinâse), and its compound *palujjati*, M. iii. 5, 9, Mahâparinibb. 40; *paloka*, 'the necessity of dissolution,' ib.; *sajjulasa*=sarjarasa, 'resin,' M. vi. 7; *elâḷuka* = ervâruka, 'cucumber,' Jât. i. 205, 312; *elaṇḍa*=eraṇḍa, 'Ricinus,' Assalâyanasutta 35; *salaḷa*=sarala, 'a flower,' Jât. i. 13; *puthuloma* =pṛithuroman, 'a fish;' the preposition *pari* in *palibodha*, 'hindrance,' which, according to Childers, is the result of a confusion between *parirodha* and *paribâdha*; *palibuddhati*, 'to hinder,' *paligha* = parigha, 'an iron beam;' *paligedha*, a compound of *gedha*, 'greed,' Ang. ii. 4, 7 (it has nothing to do with the Sinhalese pali, 'reverend,' in the Tissamahârâma inscription); *palipanna*=paripanna, 'covered,' M. viii. 26, 1; *paliguṇṭhita*, 'entangled' (also spelt *palikuṇḍhita*, Jât. ii. 92); *pâliguṇṭhima*, 'laced,' M. v. 2, 3; *paliveṭheti* = pariveshṭ, 'to wrap up,' *phâlibhadda*, Jât. ii. 163 = pâribhadra, 'the coral tree,' Prâk. *phâlihadda*, Hem. i. 232, 254; *sukhumâla* = sukumâra, 'youthful,' by amalgation with sukhuma, Trenckner 66; *agalu* =aguru, 'Agallochum;' *vâla*=vâr, 'water;' *kaṭuḷa* = kaṭura, 'buttermilk,' M. vi. 17, 1, Suttavibh. i. 66.

R is changed to *d* in *purindada*=purandara, 'a name of Indra,' also written *purinda*, Cariy. i. 9, 3, *sârandada*, 'name of a yakkha,' Mahâparin. 4; it is changed to *y* in *sâyanîya*= sâraṇîya, according to Senart Mahâvastu 599 (see above, p. 21), *mâtyâ*, *petyâ* = mâtrâ, pitrâ, Jât. 527, v. 3, 5, 528, v. 26, Trenckner, Pâli Misc. 56.

L is changed to *r* in *âkurati*, from *âkula*, 'troubled;' the Dhm. v. 94 has a verb *kura saddâdanesu*, which possibly may be identical with *âkurati*, although it is not known from any other text; *kira* = kila, 'they say;' *ârammana* = âlambana, 'support,' *arañjara*=aliñjara, 'water-jar.'

L is changed to *n* in *nalâṭa* = lalâṭa, 'forehead;' *naṅgala*= lâṅgala, 'plough;' *naṅgula* = lâṅgula, 'tail;' *dehanî* = dehalî, 'threshold;' *tintinî*=tintilî, 'the tamarind tree,' comp. *tintiṇanta*, Jâṭ. i. 243.

(8) Sibilants:—

As there is only one sibilant in Pâli, ç and sh are also represented by *s*. There are, however, a few exceptions to this rule: ç is represented by ch in *chava* = çava, 'corpse,' M. iii. 12, 7, and as an adjective 'vile,' *châpa* and *châya*, 'the young of an animal,' *cheppâ* = çepa, 'tail;' it is represented by *ḍ* in *ḍâka* = çâka, 'pot-herb,' M. vi. 35, 6; 36, 8.

H sometimes returns to its original medial aspirate, and this gives us Pâli forms which are older than the corresponding ones in Saṃskṛit: the root *nah* in composition with *api*, *ava*, *upa*, *vi*, gives *pilandhati*, *onandhati*, *upanandhati*, *vinandhati*; these forms show us that the original form of the root was *nadh* and not *nagh*, as one would feel inclined to think from comparing the Latin necto, (see Whitney's Saṃskṛit Grammar, p. 76.) Similar forms are *agghati*, 'to cast,' compared with *arahati*, *dubbhati*, 'to cheat,'=druh, Jât. i. 267, iii. 13, 192, and the adjectives belonging to the same root, *dûbhin*, Jât. ii. 386, *dûbhaka*, Jât. i. 363; *adrûbhâya*, 'truly, without falsehood,' M. x. 2, 17; *ghammati*=hammati, 'to go,' Naigh. 2, 14, Prâk. hammaï, Hem. iv. 162, Hâla 694, *ghañña*, 'destruction,' from han; the root har is found in its older form in *saṃgharitabba* v. l. to *saṃharitabba*, M. i. 25, 10. Dh. 143.

A curious change of *h* to *s* occurs in *senesika* = snaihika, 'oily,' M. vi. 1, 4, and *golisa*=goliha, 'name of a plant.'

§ 9. General Remarks referring to Consonants of Different Classes.

(1) Aspiration is very frequent in Pâli with hard and soft consonants. Instances are: *satthi*=çakti, 'ability,' *dhona*= drona, 'a measure of capacity,' Dh. 43, Fausb. S. N. 58, 149; *sukhumâla*=sukumâra, 'youthful;' *thambhakari*=stambakari, 'rice;' *kiñcikkha*=kiñcid+ka, 'some trifle;' *khaḷopi*=karoṭi, 'pot,' Mil. 107, according to Trenckner, Pâli Misc. 60 (also spelt *kalopi*); *Khandha*=Skanda, 'the god Skanda,' through confusion with *khandha*, 'shoulder;' *paccaggha* = pratyagra, 'new;' *phâliphulla*, 'in full blossom,' Jât. i. 52, Mahâparin. 53; *phâlibhadda*=pâribhadra, Jât. ii. 163; *phâsu*, 'agreeable,'= prâçu according to Trenckner, Pâli Misc. 81—I have derived it, following Paul Goldschmidt, from a hypothetical form smarçu (see my contrib. to Sinh. Gr. p. 13, note); *phâsukâ*=pârçukâ, 'a rib,' also written *pâsukâ*, C. x. 10, 1; *phussa*=pushya, 'name of a month,' and *phussita*=pushpita, 'blossoming;' *phârusaka*=parûsaka, 'Grewia Asiatica,' M. vi. 35, 6; *phalu* =paru, 'joint;' *phallava*=pallava, 'sprout,' Jât. iii. 40; *saṅkhalikâ* = saṅkalikâ, 'heap,' Jât. i. 433, Suttavibh. i. 105, Ang. p. 114, through confusion with saṅkhalikâ, 'chain,' Senart, Mahâvastu 387; the reverse process is found in Prâk., where çṛiṅkhala is changed to *saṃkala*, according to Hem. i. 189; *valabhâmukha*=vaḍabâmukha, *erâpatha*=airâvata, 'king of the Nâgas, Jât. ii. 145=C. v. 6, spelt *erapatta* Saddhammopâyana v. 349, *erakapatta*, Dh. 344; *âpâtha*=âpâta, 'path,' Trenckner, Mil. 298, M. v. 1, 25, Samanta Pâs. 300; *sunakha*, 'dog,' and *lâmakha*, 'vile,' Jât. ii. 430, are most probably older forms, as

we have the aspiration also in Prâk. suṇaho, Hem. i. 52, Pischel Beitr. vi. 92.

(2) The aspiration is dropped in *khudâ*=kshudhâ, 'hunger;' *khudita*, 'hungry;' *upâdisesa*=upadhiçesha (and with change of the position of the component parts *sesopâdi*, Dâṭh. ii. 36), Oldenberg, Buddha, p. 437, ff.; *maṭṭa*=mṛishṭa, 'polished;' *abhivaṭṭa*=abhivṛishṭa, 'wet from rain,' Mil. 176; *anovaṭṭa*, Jât. i. 18; *paṭanga* = phaḍinga, 'flying insect;' *paggava* = phalgava, from phalgu, 'herb,' Jât. ii. 105; *anaṅgaṇa*, 'free from impurity,' compared with aṅhas, 'sin,' Jainaprâk. aṇaṇhaya (E. M. Beitr. p. 33); *rajovajalla* and *rajojalla*, Ass. S. 13, Jât. i. 390, 'dust and dirt,'=rajas+jhalla, comp. Jainapr. jalla, E. M. Beitr. 34; *âvajjeti*=avadhyâ, 'to reflect,' Senart, Mahâvastu 377; a curious instance of dropped aspiration is *kâ*, Jât. ii. 258=khâ, 'spring,' Naigh., and perhaps we have to notice the same process in *kakkâreti*, 'to express disgust,' Jât. ii. 105, Five Jât. 29,=*khât* or *khâṭ*+*kâreti*, which, however, might be also derived, with Childers, from *kât*+*kâreti*. As in Greek, two aspirations are not allowed in two syllables following each other, and when this happens the first is dropped, as, e.g., *nikkaddhati*=nishkṛish, 'to cast out.'

(3) There are also instances where the aspirate drops its first part and *h* alone remains, as is done frequently in Saṃskṛit and later on in all the vernaculars. I believe, however, that a number of instances, especially those with *bh*, are only due to the bad writing of the Sinhalese, in whose alphabet *h* and *bh* are so easily confounded; M. i. 1, 3, four MSS. have the form *have*, but Buddhaghosa reads *bhave*, which shows us clearly the etymology of the word; the same process can be observed in the form *hupeyya*, M. i. 6, 9 (according to Trenckner, Pâli Misc. p. 62, a Burmese error for *huveyya*). Other instances

are *momuhato* from *momugha*, 'foolish,' Fausb. S. N. 161, *ruhira* = rudhira, 'blood,' Jât. i. 274, ii. 276, Cariy. i. 9, 13, C. vii. 3, 9; at Bhikkhunîpâc. 60, Minayeff, p. 108, reads *ruhita*, the Suttavibh. ii. 316 *rûhita* with the v. l. *rudhita*, 'boil.' *Suhita*, Jât. xx. 1, 4, quoted by Minayeff, § 43, is = Skt. suhita and not sukhita.

(4) Softening of a hard consonant, that is to say, substitution of a sonant for a surd, is frequent enough in Pâli, as in *pasada*=pṛishata, 'the spotted antelope,' Cariy. iii. 13, 2; *uda*=uta, 'or;' *ruda*=ruta, 'cry,' Jât. i. 207 (comp. ii. 388, where we have the readings *rûda* and *rûta*); *kalandaka*=kalantaka, 'squirrel;' *paṭigacca* = *paṭikacca* (v. l.) from *paṭikaroti*, 'to provide against future events,' M. i. 31, 1, Trenckner at Mil. 48, 421; *vedhati*=vyathayati, 'to tremble;' *balasata*= parasvant, 'rhinoceros,' Trenckner, P. M. 59; *sujâ*=sruc, 'a ladle;' *puñj* for *puñch*=proñch, 'to wipe,' Jât. i. 47, 318, 352. A certain instance of this change is in my opinion *jhâyati*= kshâ, 'to burn,' although Trenckner, P. M. 65, objects; I have found several new forms of this verb and its causative *jhâpeti* or *jhapeti*, in addition to those given by Childers: *jhatvâ*, Jât. ii. 262 (Comm. *kilametvâ*); *jhatta*, Mah. 146, Dh. 325; *nijjhatta*, Mil. 209, and most probably also *jâpeti*, Mil. 171, which seems to be a misprint; comp. *nijhapeti*, 'to injure,' in Açoka's pillar edict, no. iv. Cunningham, p. 112; Kern, Ind. Ant. v. 273; Prâk. jhijjai, Hem. ii. 3.

Instead of *p* we generally find *v* in this case, as in *âvelâ*= âpîḍa, 'garland;' *theva*=stepa, 'drop,' Pischel Beitr. iii. 239, vi. 102 (Hem. ii. 125 derives it from stoka); *posâvana*, 'supporting,' according to Childers=*posâpana*; *vyâvaṭa*=vyâpṛita, 'covered,' Trenckner, P. M. 63, and *veyyâvacca*, *veyyâvaṭika*, 'service.'

(5) The reverse process, hardening of a soft consonant, or substitution of a surd for a sonant, occurs in *pâyâka*=prayâga, 'sacrifice,' Jât. 543; *ajakara* = ajagara, 'the boa constrictor,' Jât. iii. 484; *kilâsu* = glâsnu, 'lazy,' Suttavibh. i. 8; *kaṭupika*, 'going up to the waist,' Jât. 119, compared with *kaṭupaga*, Suttavibh. ii. 340; *dûrûpaka*, Jât. ii. 167; *kulupika*, C. x. 13, 1; *saṃsati* for saṃsadi, loc. of saṃsad, 'congregation,' Jât. iii. 493, 495; *parisati* and *parisatiṃ*, loc. of parishad, Suttavibh. ii. 285; *kusîta* for kusîda, 'lazy,' already in the Maitrâyaṇî Saṃhitâ; *pipa*=piba, 'drink,' Jât. i. 459; *pokkharasâtaka*=pushakarasâdaka, 'name of a bird;' *dhopana*=dhovana, 'washing,' Jât. ii. 117; *laketi* = lageti, 'to stick;' and *lakanaka*, 'anchor,' Mil. 377; *thaketi*=sthagayati, 'to cover,' sometimes spelt *thakk*°., Suttavibh. ii. 54; *palikha* = paligha, 'an iron beam,' Jât. 545; *chakala* = chagala, 'goat,' Suttavibh. i. 166; *chakaṇa*=chagaṇa, 'dung,' M. vi. 9; *palikuṇṭhita*=pariguṇṭhita, 'entangled,' Jât. ii. 92; *pabbaja* = balvaja, 'reed' (spelt *babbaja*, Suttavibh. i. 90); *pappata* = parvata, 'mountain,' I. O. C. 104; *tippa* for *tibba* = tîvra, 'sharp,' Mil. 148; *tuvaṃtuva*, 'quarrel' = dvandva, through confusion with the pronoun *tvaṃ*; *pâceti* = pra+aj, 'to drive,' and *pâcana*, 'a goad,' Cariy. i. 1, 1; *sateratâ* = çatahradâ, 'lightning;' *jaṇṇutaggha*=jânudaghna, 'knee-deep,' Prâk. °thaggha, Pâiyal. 249; *Yamataggi*=Jamadagni, 'name of a ṛishi;' *vipâtikâ*=vipâdikâ, 'abscess on the foot.' The root *dhâ* in some derivations substitutes *th*, as *pithîyati*, 'is covered' = apidhîyate (for which the Burmese write *pidhîyati*); *upatheyya*, 'cushion.' A similar process with regard to the root *dhmâ* can be observed in *santhamaṃ*=sandhaman, 'blowing,' Jât. i. 122.

(6) An interchange between the different classes of mutes is not infrequent in Pâli. Instances are *kipillika* = pipîlika, 'an ant,' also written *pipîlika*, Saddhammopâyana, v. 23,

pipillika, Jât. i. 202; *takkola* = kakkola, 'Bdellium,' Jât. i. 291, also used as name of a country, Mil. 359, where it most probably corresponds to Skt. Karkoṭa; *jalûpikâ* = jalûkikâ, 'a leech,' Mil. 407, originally jalauka, 'living in the water;' *khajjopanaka* = khadyota, 'the fire-fly,' Dh. 338, Dâṭh. iii., 78; *gaddûhana* = dadrûghna, 'a small measure of space or time,' Trenckner, P. M. 89; *kaḷopi* = karoṭi (written *khaḷopi*, Mil. 107, Ab. 456), 'a pot;' *âlupa* = âluka, 'ebony,' Jât. 446, v. 1; *chiggala* = chidra + la, 'hole,' Childers, s. v. tâḷa, *Pakudha* = Kakudha, C. v. 8, 1. In most of these cases the reason of the change is dissimilation, as we find it also in *phâsulikâ* = pârçukâ + ika, 'a rib,' M. i. 61, 1; *sallalîkata* = çalyakîkṛita, 'pierced,' Jât. i. 180. Other instances are not quite so easy to explain, such as *rumbh* for rudh in *sannirumbhitvâ*, Jât. i. 62, 80, 163, ii. 6 (v. l. *sannirujjhitvâ*), comp. Fausböll, Ten Jât. 93, and *sakk* if this is really = sarp, as Trenckner, P. M. 60, believes; perhaps we ought to derive it from caṅkram with a similar abbreviation of the reduplicated root, as in *jaggati* for *jâgarati*, but I give this merely as a hypothesis. The change of *c* to *s* would make no difficulty; the dissimilation adduced by Trenckner does not hold good for all instances, as in *osakkati*, *ussakkati*, *nissakkati*, *visakkiya*, Suttavibh. i. 74, we have no *p* in the prepositions; comp. also Prâk. osakka, 'departed,' Pâiyal. 178. *Khâṇu*, 'the stump of a tree,' is rightly referred to Skt. sthâṇu by the Prâk. grammarians Vararuci and Hemacandra, and the same change of sth to kh is also adopted for the explanation of duḥkha = duḥstha by Jacobi K. Z. xxv. 438 ff., comp. Ascoli 236. *Chambhati* is derived from stambh, 'to tremble,' by Trenckner; Ascoli, p. 256, rejects this derivation, but does not suggest any other instead. From the Saṃskṛit of the northern Buddhists we might compare icchattam = itthattam 'existence,' Mahâvastu, 417.

§ 10. Consonants Added or Dropped.

A consonant is dropped in the beginning of a word in *ûkâ* or *ûka* = yûka, 'louse,' Prâk. ûkâ, Pischel Beitr. iii. 241.

A consonant is added at the beginning of some verbal forms commencing with a *u*, which originates from Samprasâraṇa, as in *vuccati* = ucyate, *vutta* = upta, 'sown,' Mil. 375; *vuttha* and *vusita* from vasati, 'to dwell;' *vusîmat*, 'accomplished,' Fausböll, S. N. 208. This euphonic *v* is not only used after vowels but also after anusvâra, and sometimes even at the beginning of a line, as in *vuṭṭhahante*, Mah. 30. Where the *u* is long, we have to assume two prepositions, as in *vûpasamati* = vyupa°, comp. Senart, Mahâvastu, p. 441, and the same where the *v* is followed by *o*, as in *vokkamati* = vyutkram°, Hem. i. 116; and Pischel's remarks, *avossajiṃsu*, Dâṭh. iii. 15.

In the middle of a word consonants are often elided through Samprasâraṇa. The syllable *ya* is contracted to *i* in *mahâbodhiṅgana* = mahâbodhyaṅgana, 'the yard of the great Bo tree,' Mah. 176; *paṭiviṃsa* or *paṭivisa*, 'portion,' = *pratyaṃça*; *aticchatha*, 'go further on,' from *ati* + *acch*; *nibbijjhati* = nirvyadh, 'to pierce;' *saccika* = satyaka, 'true,' Mil. 226; *pattiya* = pratyaya and *pattiyâyati*, 'to believe,' Jât. i. 426 v. l.; it is contracted to *e* in *vedhati* = vyath, 'to tremble;' to *î* in *vîtivatta* = vyativṛitta, 'having passed;' *avîvadâta* = avyavadâta, 'confused,' Fausböll, S. N. 149; *vîtihâra* = vyatihâra, 'long step.'

The syllable *yâ* is contracted to *î* in *visîveti* = viçyâpayati, 'to warm oneself,' sometimes written *visibbeti* through confusion with *visibbati*, 'to unsew,' e. g., M. i. 20, 15 Pât. 15, Suttavibh. ii. 115; from the same root *âsîyati* = âçyâyati, 'to cool oneself,' Mil. 75; *thîna* = styâna, 'idleness,' but *patthinna*, 'stiff,' M. viii. 11, 2; to *i* in *anabhijjhita* = anabhidhyâta, 'not coveted,' M. viii. 12, 2, where, however, the *y* is also contained in the group *jjh*; to *e* in *jeyyo*=jyâyas, 'better;' *ajjheyyaka* = âdhyâyaka, 'teacher,' Rasavâhinî 19.

The syllable *va* is contracted to *u* in *supina* = svapna, 'sleep;' *turita* = tvarita, 'hasty;' *kuthita*, 'cooked,' from kvath, Vinaya texts, ii. 57; it remains doubtful whether the root *kuth*, 'to be distressed,' Dhm. Mil. 250, Suttav. i. 108, is the same; Dh. 155 we have *koddhetvâ*, 'having cooked;' to *o* in *sobbhânu* = svarbhânu, 'the ascending node;' *sobbha* = çvabhra, 'hole,' and *kussobbha*, 'small water,' Fausböll, S. N. 131; to *û* in *catûha* = catu+ahan, 'four days,' M. i. 72, 2.

The syllable *vâ* is contracted to *u* in *laṭukikâ* from laṭvâka, 'quail;' the syllable *vi* in *duratta* = dvirâtra, 'two nights.' *Dohaḷinî*, which Kacc. 203 also considers as a compound of dvi, has nothing to do with this numeral.

Ayà and *ayi* are contracted to *e* in a great number of causative verbs and also in a few primitives, as *apasseti* = apâçrayati, 'to lean,' C. vi. 20, 2; *neti* = nayati, 'to lead;' *apassena* = apâçrayana; *ajjhena* = adhyayana, 'reading,' Jât. iii. 114, Fausböll, S. N. 40; *acceka* = atyayika, 'accidental.' *Aya* and *âya* are contracted to *e* in *paleti* = palâyati, 'to flee;' to *â* in *Kâtiyânî* and *Kaccânî*=Kâṭyâyanî, Jât. iii. 427; *Moggallâna*= Maudgalyâyana, *ekânika* = ekâyanika, Mil. 402; *upaṭṭhâka* = upaṭṭhâyaka, 'servant,' also written *upaṭṭhaka* with ă, Bv. ii. 70; *patisallâṇa* = pratisaṃlayana, 'solitude;' *abbhâna* = abhyayana, 'rehabilitation;' *upajjha* = upâdhyâya, 'preceptor;' *abhiññâ* = abhijñâya, 'having known;' *paṭisaṅkhâ* = pratisaṅkhyâya, 'having reflected.'

The group *ariya* is first changed to *ayira* and then contracted to *era* in *âcera* = âcârya, 'teacher,' Khuddasikkhâ; or to *îra*, as in *parihîrati*=parihāryati; *asaṃhîra* = asamharya, 'unconquerable,' Dîp. 31.

Iya is contracted to *i* in *kittaka*=kiyattaka, from kiyant, 'how much;' to *e* in *etta*, *ettaka*=iyatta, from iyant, Mahâvastu, p. 384; in Prâk. we have kettia and ettia, Hem. ii. 157, Goldschmidt, Prâkritica, p. 23. Trenckner takes *etta* to be abridged from *ettaka*, Pâli Misc. 65, note 23.

Ava is contracted to *o* very often in compounds formed with the preposition ava, as *onîta*=avanîta, 'cleansed,' in the phrase *onîtapattapâṇi*, frequent in the Vinaya, see Vinaya Texts i. 83; *ojahati*=avahâ, 'to forsake,' aorist passive *ohiyi*, Dh. 158, *ohiyyaka*, 'left behind,' Suttavibh. i. 208; *odahati* = avadhâ, 'to deposit;' *vossagga*=vyavasarga, Lotus, 312, and *avossajjiṃsu*, Dâṭh. iii. 15; *ogadha*=avagâdha, 'belonging to;' *ora* = avara and avâra, 'lower' and 'hither;' *opatta*=avapattra, 'without leaves,' Jât. iii. 496; *uddosita*=udavasita, 'stable,' M. iii. 5, 9, C. x. 24, Suttavibh. i. 200, Ab. 213. Other instances are *pahonaka* = prabhavanaka, 'sufficient,' and *pâhuna* = prabhavana, Mah. 205; *poṇa* = pravaṇa, 'sloping;' *opeti* = âvapati, 'to put,' Trenckner, Pâli Misc. 78; *osâpeti* causative of âviç, 'to sling,' Jât. i. 25. In *anavaya* = anavayava, 'perfectly versed in,' Mil. 10, and *appatissa*=appatissava, Jât. i. 217, the last syllable is dropped because the word was too long.

Instead of *o* we also find *u* in the same or similar cases, as *ûhadati*=avahad, 'to befoul with excrement' (see above, p. 15); *ujjhâyati* = avadhyâ, 'to be annoyed;' *uññâ* = avajñâ, 'contempt,' and *uññâtabba*, Feer. Et. Bouddh. 128; *âhuneyya* = âhavanîya, Mahâparin. 20 comp. the commentary to Ang. ii. 4, 4.

The group *apa* can undergo the same changes as *ava*, and it is sometimes difficult to find out which preposition we must assume as the corresponding Saṃskṛit word: *ovaraka*=apavaraka, 'store-room,' Jât. i. 391; *oggata*=apagata in *oggate suriye*, 'after sunset,' Suttavibh. ii. 268, *ottappa* = apatrâpya, 'fear of sinning,' Senart, Mahâvastu 463.

Other contractions have taken place in *oka*=udaka, 'water;' *Kuçinârâ* = Kuçinagara; *koṭṭhaka* = koyashṭika, 'paddy bird,' Five Jât. 36; *jantaggha*=yantragṛiha, 'bath-room,' Suttavibh. i. 55; *paccûsamaya* = *paccûsasamaya*, 'morning;' *chaṅgula* = shaḍaṅgula, 'six inches,' Mah. 211; *pavissâmi* for *pavisissâmi*, Jât. ii. 68; *sosârita*=su + osârita; *dosârita*=durosârita, 'duly and unduly restored,' M. ix. 4, 11; *vivicchâ* = vicikicchâ, 'doubt;' *dûpadhârita* = durupadh°, Suttavibh. ii. 275, the opposite to *sûpadhârita*, 'well kept in mind,' M. v. 13, 9.

Metathesis is very frequent in Sinhalese, see my Contrib. to Sinh. Grammar, p. 14; in Pâli we have only a few instances, as *upâhanâ*=upânah, 'shoe;' *pârupana* for pâvaraṇa or pâvurana, Suttavibh. i. 180, 'upper robe,' see Pischel, Beitr. iii. 247; *kasaṭa*=sakaṭa, 'insipid,' Mil. 119, Dh. 275, Jât. ii. 97, Ang. ii. 5, 5; *cilimikâ*, C. vi. 2, 6 and *cimilikâ*, Suttavibh. ii. 40, most probably go back to a form cilamîlikâ or ciliminikâ, 'an ornament,' Vyut. 208, comp. Vinaya texts ii. 153.

§ 11. Changes of Consonants at the End of a Word.

According to the rule given above, p. 23, we only find vowels or nasals at the end of a Pâli word. Every nasal is changed into anusvâra and a preceding long vowel shortened in consequence. Very often the anusvâra is dropped altogether especially in verse when a short syllable is required by the metre, as *etaṃ, buddhâna sâsanaṃ* = etad buddhânâm çâsanam, 'this is the command of the Buddhas,' Dh. v. 183. Other cases will be treated of in the chapter on Sandhi.

Before a word beginning with a consonant the anusvâra can be changed into the nasal of the corresponding class, as in *hiriṅ taraṅtaṃ*, Jât. iii. 196. Before a word beginning with a vowel the anusvâra may be changed into *m*, as in *caram atandito* for caran=carant, Dh. v. 305.

The termination *as* generally becomes *o* whatever the consonant beginning the next word may be, as in the nom. sing. of *a*—stems almost regularly. There are a few exceptions to this rule which are considered as Mâgadhisms by most grammarians. A passage of this kind occurs in the Sâmaññaphalasutta Gr. p. 121, *n'atthi attakâre n'atthi parakâre n'atthi purisakâre*, 'there is no action on our part, there is no action on the part of others, there is no human action.' Another Mâgadhizing passage from Majjhima Nikâya is quoted by Trenckner, Pâli Misc. p. 75: *ânañjâdhimuttassa purisapuggalassa ye lokâmisasaññojane se vante*, where we find the *e* used for a neuter noun. I feel sure that a more careful study of Pâli literature will furnish us a great many more passages of this kind. They all agree in this point, that the nom. in *e* is only formed of stems in *a* and never of any consonantal stems, the same rule which holds good for the Jainaprâkṛit, see E. M. Beitr. zur Gram. d. Jainapr. p. 38. About the origin of this *e* several opinions have been advanced, but I will not discuss them here, as the subject belongs more especially to Prâkṛit grammar. The vocatives *bhante* and *bhikkhave* are taken over directly from the Mâgadhî.

Besides these nominatives in *e* we have several adverbs terminating in *as*, which change the *as* to *e*, as *suve*=çvaḥ, 'tomorrow;' *tadahe*=tadahas, 'on that day,' which also occurs in the form *tadahu*; *atippage* (and *atippago*)=atiprâgaḥ, Senart, Mahâvastu 418, most probably also *tâvade*, *yâvade*, which, however, are explained by Childers as abridged forms of *tâvadeva*, *yâvadeva*.

The *s* is dropped and the *a* alone remains in *okamokata* for okamokatas, 'from the water,' Dh. v. 34; *tâvatiṃsa* = trayastṛimça, 'thirty-three;' and with lengthening of the *a*, *rajâpatha* = rajaḥpatha, 'dust-hole;' *jarâmaraṇa* = jaras + maraṇa, 'decay and death.'

The syllable *as* is changed to *u* through an intermediate *o* in *tadahu*, *mithu*=mithas, 'mutually;' *mithubheda*, M. vi. 28, 8; *sajju*=sadyas, 'instantly.'

Other consonants at the end of a word are simply dropped, and the remaining vowel generally is not changed. There are, however, some cases where it is lengthened, shortened, or a nasal is added:—

(1) It is lengthened in *dhî* = dhik, 'fie;' *brahâ* = bṛihat, 'mighty;' *parisâ*=parishad, 'assembly.'

(2) It is shortened, as in *kayira* for *kayirâ* = kuryât, Das., Jât. 28; *assa*=syât, &c.

(3) A nasal is added, as in the verbal terminations *uṃ*=us, *eyyuṃ*=eyyus, *isuṃ*=ishus, *sanaṃ*=sanat, 'always;' *saniṃ*= çanais, 'slowly' or 'quickly,' Mah. 156; *visuṃ* = vishvak, 'separately;' *khattuṃ*=kṛitvas, a form which occurs also in the Saṃskṛit of the northern Buddhists, see Senart, Mahâvastu 541; *manaṃ* = manâk, 'nearly,' Jât. i. 149, M. ii. 12, 1, the same form in Prâk. Hem. ii. 169; *tiriyaṃ*=tiryak, 'across.'

§ 12. Compound Consonants.

Compound consonants are generally assimilated, as in all Prâkṛit dialects. Sometimes the assimilation is avoided by inserting a vowel, as we have seen above, p. 12. In the beginning of a word, instead of a double surd or sonant resulting from assimilation, a single surd or sonant is written, and instead of a surd or sonant aspirate only the aspirate.

The assimilation is generally progressive, so that the first consonant is assimilated to the second, especially so with explosives.

Kt becomes *tt* in *mutta*=mukta, 'released' (but *kk* in *paṭimukka*, 'fixed'); *satti*=çakti, 'power' (also written *satthi*); *sattu*=çaktu, 'barley' (also written *satthu* at Pât. 89); *sippi* 'pearl oyster,' which Trenckner, Pâli Misc. 60, identifies with *çukti*, I believe to be borrowed from some vernacular language.

Kth becomes *tth*, as *satthi*=çakthi, 'thigh.'

Gdh becomes *ddh*, as in *duddha*=dugdha, 'milk.'

G+*bh*=*bbh*: *pabbhâra*=prâgbhâra, 'a cave.'

Ḍ+*g*=*gg*: *khagga*=khaḍga, 'a sword.'

T+*k*=*kk*: *ukkâra*=utkâra, 'dung.'

T+*p*=*pp*: *uppatati*=utpat, 'to jump.'

D+*g*=*gg*: *puggala*=pudgala, 'individual.'

D+*gh*=*ggh*: *uggharati*=ud+ghṛi, 'to ooze.'

D+*b*=*bb*: *bubbula*=budbuda, 'a bubble.'

D+*bh*=*bbh*: *ubbhijjati*=ud+bhid, 'to burst;' *ubbhitodaka* =udbhṛitodaka, Gr. 140.

P+*t*=*tt*: *vutta*=upta, 'shaven.'

B+*j*=*jj*: *paṭikujjeti*=prati+kubj, 'to cover,' Jât. i. 50, 69, Mahâparin. 56, Mahâvastu 377.

B+d=dd: *sadda*=çabda, 'a sound.'

B+dh=ddh: *laddha*=labdha, 'taken.'

When an explosive meets a following nasal the assimilation is generally retrogressive, or is avoided by the insertion of a vowel. There are, however, some instances also of progressive assimilation :—

K+n becomes *kk* in *sakkoti* or *sakkuṇâti* (where the double *k* can only be explained by false analogy)=çaknoti, 'to be able;' *kukkusa*=kiknasa, 'grain,' C. x. 27, 4.

K+m = mm: *rummavatî* = rukmavatî, 'name of a verse,' Vuttod. ap. Fryer, Pâli Studies, p. 8.

G+n=gg in *aggi* or *aggini*=agni, 'fire,' Kacc. 54, Jât. iii. 320; gini, S. N. 3.

Gh+n=ggh: *viggha*=vighna, 'obstacle.'

J+n=ññ: *aññâ*=âjñâ, 'order.' [In *oñâta* and *avañâta*= avajâta, 'low born,' Pât. 83, and *kolañña*=kulaja, 'high born,' Mil. 256, the roots *jan* and *jñâ* are confounded.]

Ḍ+m: *kuḍumala*=kuḍmala, 'a bud.'

T+n: *sapattî* = sapatnî, 'hostile,' but *gahapatânî* = gṛihapatnî, 'house-wife,' *ratana*=ratna, 'jewel.'

T+m: *attâ* and *âtumâ*=âtmâ, 'self;' *tumo*=tmanâ, Oldenberg K. Z. xxv. 319.

Th+n=tth: *abhimatthati*=abhimathnâti, 'to grind.'

D+m: *chadda*=chadman, 'roof;' *paduma*=padma, 'lotus;' *dammi*=dadmi, 'I give.'

Dh+n: *bunda*=budhna, 'the root of a tree.'

Dh+m: *idhuma* = idhma, 'fire-wood;' *veṇudhama* = veṇudhma, 'a flute-player;' and from the same root *uddhumâyati*= uddhmâ, 'to be blown up.'

P+n: *pappoti* and *pâpuṇâti*=prâpnoti, 'to obtain;' *supina* and *soppa*=svapna, 'sleep.'

P+m: *pâpimâ*=pâpman, 'sinful.'

Groups containing a nasal and following explosive generally remain unchanged; the following are exceptions:—

Nc becomes *ññ* in *paññâsa* = pañcâçat, 'fifty;' *ṇṇ* in *paṇṇuvîsam* = pañcaviṃçati, 'twenty-five,' Jât. iii. 138; *nn* in *pannarasa*, 'fifteen,' *paṇṇarasî*, 'the day of the full or new moon,' comp. Sinh. panas, Prâk. paṇavaṇṇâ, Pischel, Beitr. iii. 245.

Nj becomes *ññ* in *viññitvâ* and *viññâpetvâ* from vṛiñj, Suttavibh. ii. 264, but *âviñji*, Suttavibh. i. 127, *âviñjanâ*, ib. 121, and with hardening of the *j* to *ch*, *âviñchanâ*, C. v. 14, 3, 4.

Nḍ becomes *ṇṇ* in *puṇṇarika* = puṇḍarîka, 'lotus,' in a passage of the Ang. quoted by Oldenberg, Buddha 424; simplified in *bhâṇaka*=bhâṇḍaka, 'a jar;' *ḍḍ* in *deḍḍubha*=duṇḍubha, 'a kind of lizard.'

Mb becomes *mm* in *ammâ* = ambâ, 'mother;' *ârammana* = âlambana, 'support.'

When two nasals meet progressive assimilation takes place, as in *ummagga* = unmârga, 'an underground watercourse,' *ninna*=nimna, 'deep.'

Groups containing *y* generally assimilate the same to the other element. If, however, the first element is a dental the whole group passes into the palatal class. In many cases the assimilation is avoided by the insertion of an *i* or the group remains unchanged.

(1) Gutturals: *ussukka* = autsukya, 'zeal;' *sokhiya* = saukhya, 'happiness;' *âkhyâta*=âkhyâta, 'announced;' *yogga* =yogya, 'proper.'

(2) Palatals: *vuccati* = ucyate, pass. of vac; *joti* = jyotis, 'light;' *jiyâ* and *jyâ* = jyâ, 'the bow-string;' and *adejjha* = adhijya, Jât. iii. 274.

(3) Cerebrals: *kuḍḍa* = kuḍya, 'a wall;' *âḍhya*, *aḍḍha* = âḍhya, 'rich;' *puñña*=puṇya, 'good.'

(4) Dentals: *âhacca* = âhṛitya for âhârya, 'having told;' *ûhacca*=avahadya, 'having befouled;' *ekacca*=ekatya, 'a certain,' according to Senart, Mahâvastu 388, comp. *ekacciya*, M. viii. 14, 2 (Childers and Trenckner, Pâli Misc. 56 derive it from ekatara); *âvajjati*=avadhyâ, 'to consider;' *añña*=anya, 'other;' *cicca* = cintya for cintayitvâ. The assimilation does not take place in *cetya*, *cetiya* = caitya, 'a relic-shrine;' *vyattaya* = vyatyaya, 'opposition;' *paṭaggi* = pratyagni, 'fire in return;' *pâṭaṅkî* = pratyaṅkin, 'a sedan chair,' M. viii. 10, 3; *pâṭekka* from pratyeka, 'singly' (the regular form *pacceka* occurs frequently); *pasîdiya* = prasîdya, 'believing,' Mah. 5; in compositions with *ud* we obtain the group *yy*, as *uyyoga* = udyoga, 'departure.'

(5) Labials: *tappati*=tapyate, pass. of tap; *labbhati*=labhyate, pass. of labh; *lepya*=lepya, 'plastering.'

(6) After *r* we generally find epenthesis, as in *âcariya* = âcârya, 'teacher;' *suriya* = sûrya, 'sun;' and sometimes the position of the sounds is inverted so that we have the group *yir* instead of the group *riy*, as in *ayira* = ârya, Jât. ii. 349; *bhayirâ*=bhâryâ, 'wife;' *kayirâ*=kuryât optative, and *kayirati* =kriyate, passive of kar. Besides, we have cases of retrogressive and progressive assimilation; when retrogressive assimilation takes place we get the group *yy* and sometimes a single *y*, when progressive assimilation, we obtain a single *r*, as this consonant cannot be doubled, with a long vowel before it. Instances are: *ayya* = ârya, 'noble;' *jiyyati*, *jîyati*, and *jîrati*=jar, 'to grow old;' *seyyasi*=çîryasi, from çar, 'to decay,' Jât. i. 174, Dh. 147; *paripûrati* = paripûryate, 'to be filled.' The group *ry* is changed to *ll* in *vipallâsa*=viparyâsa, 'change,'

Suttavibh. i. 7: *pallaṅka* = paryaṅka, 'couch;' *pallattha* = paryasta, 'posture,' Jât. i. 163.

L+y is either preserved or assimilated: *kalyâṇa* and *kallâṇa* = kalyâna, 'fortunate.'

V+y is often written *by* in the beginning of a word where it represents the preposition *vi*; this is the spelling of the Burmese MSS. while the Sinhalese write *vy*; in a few instances I have found it in the middle of a word, viz. *korabya* = kauravya, Jât. ii. 371; *upasambyâna* = upasaṃvyâna, 'the outer garment,' Ab. 292. We also find examples of assimilation in the beginning, as *vavatthâpeti* = vyavasthâpayati, 'to settle;' *vâyamati* = vyâyam, 'to struggle;' *vodaka* = vyudaka, 'without water;' *vossajjati* = vyavasṛij, 'to relinquish.' In the middle of a word *vy* remains as in *pathavyâ*, Dh. 32, or is divided by *i*, as in *puthuviyâ*, Mah. 19, *puthuviyaṃ*, Att. 8; it may however also be assimilated to *bb*, as in *abbocchinna* = avyavachinna, 'unbroken,' Mil. 72; *abbohârika* = avyavahârika, Suttavibh. i. 91; *bhâtubba* = bhrâtṛivya, 'cousin,' Bâlâvatâra, p. 36; *abhabba* = abhavya, 'unable;' *sibbati* = sîvyati, 'to sew;' *pasibbaka*, 'a bag,' from the same root. The *y* is altogether dropped in *gâvuta* = gavyûti, 'a measure of length.' The forms in *tayya* = tavya, given by the Grammarians as *ñâtayya* = jñâtavya, *pattayya* = prâptavya, I believe do not belong to the living language. After a sibilant we have progressive assimilation; the only exception is *âlasya* or *âlasiya* = âlasya, 'sloth,' Dh. 40.

In the group *hy* the position of the elements is reversed, so that it becomes *yh*, as *mayhaṃ* = mahyam; exceptions are *bâhya*, 'external' (also *bâhira* with change of *y* to *r*) and *etihya* = aitihya, 'oral tradition,' Ascoli 244. Assimilation takes place in *leyya* = lehya, 'to be licked;' epenthesis in *hiyyo* or *hîyo* = hyas, 'yesterday.' For *yh* in *vuyhati* = uhyate we also find *ḷh*: *vuḷhati* (Ascoli 244 derives this from the part. *vûḷha*, I doubt whether the form is correct).

R before an explosive is always assimilated, and if the explosive is a dental the group may become cerebral; in a few instances also the influence of the *r* is shown by aspiration.

(1) Gutturals: *sakkharâ* = çarkarâ, 'sugar,' spelt *sakkarâ*, Jât. i. 238; *vagga*=varga, 'class;' *dîgha*=dîrgha, 'long,' with compensation; *kakkasa*=karkaça, 'rough.'

(2) Palatals: *acci* = arci, 'flame,' spelt *acchi* in a passage of Saṃyuttaka Nikâya quoted by Oldenberg, Buddha 434; *mucchati* = mûrchati, 'to faint;' *sajja* = sarja, 'the sal tree.'

(3) Cerebrals: *kaṇṇa*=karṇa, 'the ear;' *kaṇṇakita*=karṇakṛita, Suttavibh. ii. 282.

(4) Dentals: *pârivaṭṭaka* = parivartaka, 'a robe lent to a priest and returned by him after a period,' Pât. 8. 13. 78, but *pârivattaka* Suttavibh. ii. 59; *âvaṭṭa*=âvarta, 'whirlpool,' Mah. 213, but *âvatta*, Jât. i. 70; *vaṭṭaka*=vartaka, 'quail;' *vaṭṭati*= vartati, 'to be right,' but *âvattati* and *nibbattati*; *attha* = artha, 'reason,' but *aṭṭa*, 'lawsuit;' *kevaṭṭa*=kaivarta, 'fisher,' also spelt *keraṭṭha* in Wastergaard's Catalogue 21*a*; *chaḍḍeti* =chard, 'to throw away,' also spelt *chaḍḍh*, Jât. i. 277; *parimaddati* = parimard, 'to excel,' also spelt *parimaddh*, Jât. i. 145; *addita* = ardita, 'afflicted,' Mah. 3, but *aḍḍita*, Bv. ii. 129; *daḍḍhi*=darḍhya, 'sloth,' Trenckner, Pâli Misc. 65. A curious metathesis takes place in *gadrabha* = gardabha, 'a donkey,' but in *gaddabhaṇḍa*=gardabhâṇḍa, 'the tree Thespesia populneoides,' the assimilation is regular.

(5) Labials: *kappûra* = karpûra, 'camphor;' *abbuda* = arbuda, 'a high number;' *gabbha* = garbha, 'womb;' *kamma* = karma, 'action.' The group *rv* becomes *bb*, as in *pabbaha* =

parvata (spelt *pappata* sometimes in Burmese MSS.); *cappeti* =carv, 'to chew,' C. 317.

(6) Sibilants: assimilation in *dassana* = darçana, 'sight;' epenthesis in *arisa* = arças, 'hemorrhoids;' *ârissa* = ârsha, 'ṛishiship,' Kacc. 216. The group *rsh* is turned into *h* in *kahâpana* = karshâpaṇa, *kâhiti* = kârshyati. From barsh we have a present *haṃsati*, 'to rejoice,' Suttavibh. i. 8, Kacc. 390.

(7) Before *h* we always have epenthesis, as in *arahati* = arhati, *barihisa*=barhis, 'sacrificial grass.'

R following an explosive is also generally assimilated, but here we find several instances where it is retained or a vowel is inserted:—

(1) Gutturals: *vakka*=vakra, 'crooked;' *khiḍḍâ* (and *kîḷâ*) =krîḍâ, 'play;' *khuṃseti* = kruç, 'to curse,' comp. Pischel, Beitr. iii. 253; *vagga* = vyagra, 'irregular,' Oldenberg K. Z. xxv. 324; *paccaggha*=pratyagra, 'new;' with epenthesis *kiriyâ* =kriyâ, 'deed;' *kurûra*=krûra, 'cruel.'

(2) Palatals: *vajira*=vajra, 'thunder-bolt.'

(3) Dentals: *sattu* = çatru, 'enemy,' spelt *satthu*, Dîp. 21; *sâvitthî* = sâvitrî, M. vi. 35, 8, spelt *sâvittî*, Fausb. S. N. 75; *tattha*, *yattha*, *kattha* = tatra, yatra, kutra, 'there,' 'where,' *parattha*=paratra, 'elsewhere;' *sotthiya*=çrotriya, 'a brahmin;' *sabbathattâ*=sarvatratvât, 'in every way,' according to Weber, Indische Streifen iii. 397; *haliddi* = haridrî, 'turmeric myrobolan,' Suttavibh. ii. 35, spelt *haliddhi*, C. 317. The *r* is retained in *utrâsa* = uttrâsa, 'terror,' Jât. ii. 336, participle *utrasta*, Mil. 23, and *utrassa*, M. x. 2, 16 (*uttasati* occurs Att. 205, Jât. i. 326, *uttasta*, Jât. i. 414); *dudrabhi* = dundubhi, 'drum;' *yâtrâ* = yâtrâ, 'expedition;' *adrûbha*, 'undeceitful,' M. x. 2, 17 (*adûbha*, Jât. i. 180). The group *dr* is changed to *nd* in *sanda*=sâdra, 'coarse,' to *jj* in *khujja*=kshudra,

'small,' Saddhammop. 93; *dhr* to *jjh* in *gijjha*=gṛidhra 'vulture.'

(4) Labials: After *p* the *r* is assimilated, as in *piya*=priya, 'dear;' *pati* = prati, 'in return;' *phositum* from prush, 'to sprinkle,' M. vi. 14, 5, *parippositvâ*, M. i. 25, 15, *paripphosaka*, Gr. 140. *Br* is generally retained, as in *bravîti*, from brû, 'to speak,' *brahman*; *bhr* is assimilated, as in *sobbha* = çvabhra 'cave; *mr* only in the beginning of a word, as *miyyati* = mriyate; in the middle a *b* is developed out of the *m* after which the *r* disappears: *amba* = âmra, 'mango;' *tamba* = tâmra, 'copper.' *Vr* is assimilated to *v* in the beginning, and to *bb* in the middle of a word: *vajati*=vrajati, 'to go,' but *giribbaja*; *abbuta*=avrata or avṛita, 'undisciplined,' Dh. 47.

R, after a sibilant, is generally assimilated, as in *sâvaka*= çrâvaka, 'a pupil;' *massu*=çmaçru, 'beard;' epenthesis takes place in *siri*=çrî, 'glory;' *daḍḍha* and *uḍḍha* are=dasra and usrâ according to Kacc. 333, but Weber Indische Streifen iii. 370, identifies them with daṃshṭrâ and ushṭra.

Hr is assimilated in *hesa* = hresha, 'neighing;' *sateratâ*= çatahradâ, 'hail;' *rassa* = hrasva, 'short;' separated in *hirî*= hrî, 'shame;' but *hîḷita* = hrîta and *hîḷeti*, Jât. ii. 258, *rahada* =hrada, 'pond.'

L is on the whole treated very much like *r*; before gutturals and labials it is assimilated; *vagguḷî*=valgulî, 'bat,' C. vi. 2, 2, Jât. i. 493; *kiñjakkha*=kiñjalka, 'a filament;' *kappa*=kalpa, 'time;' *pagabbha*=pragalbha, 'bold;' *jamma*=jâlma, 'reckless.' Exceptions are *suṅka* = çulka, 'tribute;' *suṅkaghâta*, 'smuggling,' Suttavibh. i. 47; *gumba* = gulma, 'thicket;' *simbalî* = çâlmalî, 'the silk-cotton tree.' *Lv* is assimilated to *bb* in *kibbisa*=kilvisha, 'fault;' to *ll* in *khallâṭa*=khalvâṭa, 'bald;' *billa* and *bella*, Jât. iii. 76,=vilva, 'the Vilva tree,' but *beluva*=vailva

L after gutturals and labials is generally separated by *i*, as in *kilissati*=kliçyati (but *parikissati*, Fausb. S. N. xi.); *kilomaka*= kloman, 'the pleura,' Mil. 26; *klesa*, without epenthesis, occurs Dh. v. 88; *pilavati*=plavati, Dh. 59, Dîp. 56; *vipalâvita*, Jât. i. 326; *piluvati*, Mah. 230; *pilakkha*=plaksha, 'ficus infectoria,' Suttavibh. ii. 35, Jât. iii. 24; *pilotikâ*=plota, 'a cloth;' *pihaka* = plîhan, 'the spleen;' *ambila* = amla, 'sour;' *milakkha* = mleccha, 'a barbarian,' originally mlaska.

Rl gives *ll*, as in *dullabha*=durlabha, 'difficult to obtain.'

L after sibilants and *h* is generally separated by *i*, as in *silâghâ* = çlâghâ, 'praise;' *silesuma* and *semha* = çleshman, 'phlegm;' *hilâdati*=hlâd, 'to be glad.'

V after gutturals, palatals and cerebals, is assimilated, as in *pakka*=pakva, 'ripe;' *kaṭhati*=kvath, 'to boil;' (also written *kuth*, Vinaya texts, ii. 57, and *koddh*, Dh. 155), *jalati*=jvalati, 'to blaze;' *kiṇṇa*=kiṇva, 'yeast.'

After dentals it is also generally assimilated, as in *cattâro*= catvâras, 'four;' *taco*=tvac, 'bark, skin,' comp., however, *saṇhavâka*=çlakshṇatvak, Dh. 412; it remains unchanged in the suffix tvâ or tvâṇa, in *iritvija*=ṛitvij, 'the officiating priest;' and in the pronoun of the second person *tvaṃ*, which is also found as *tuvaṃ* and *taṃ*. *Tv* is changed into *cc* in *caccara*= catvara, 'court;' *anuvicca*=anuviditvâ (comm. jânitvâ), Dh. 41, Jât. i. 459, Fausb. S. N. xi. 91. *Dv* is assimilated in *dîpa* = dvîpa, 'island;' *uddâpa* = udvâpa, 'foundation of a wall' Mahâparin. 11; *ubbâsiyati* = udvas, 'to chase;' which is the correct reading at Mah. 45 for *ubbâhiyati*; it remains unchanged in *dve*, 'two' (also *duve*, but *bâ* = dvâ in *bârasa*, 'twelve'); *dvâra*, 'door;' *advejjha* = advaidhya, 'sincere,' Bv. ii. 110. *Dhv* is assimilated to *ddh*, as in *addhâ*=adhvan, 'road;' to *jjh* in *majjhâru*, M. v. 13, 6, probably = madhvâlu, 'yam.'

Nv is changed to *mm* in *dhammantari*=dhanvantari, Mil. 272; *daḷhadhamma* = dṛiḍhadhanva, Trenckner, P. M. 60 (but *gaṇḍîvadhanvâ*, Kacc. 182), comp. Prâk. dhamma, 'bow, Pâiyal. 37.

After a sibilant *v* is generally assimilated, as in *assa* = açva, 'a horse;' *sâmi*=svâmin, 'lord,' but also *suvâmi*, Fausb. S. N. xi., *suvâmini*, Jât. iii. 288; it remains unchanged in *svâna* (or *sâna*, *suvâna*), = çvâ, 'a dog;' *sve* (and *suve*), = çvas, 'to-morrow;' *ehisvâgata*, 'come and be welcome,' C. i. 13, 3, Suttavibh. i. 181. Epenthesis in *suvatthi* = svasti, 'welfare.'

Hv undergoes metathesis like *hy*, as in *jivhâ*=jihvâ, 'tongue; sometimes it becomes *bbh*, as in *gabbhara*=gahvara, 'a cavern.'

A sibilant preceding or following an explosive is assimilated by the same and generally produces aspiration of the group.

Ksh is mostly changed to *kkh* or *cch*, as in *cakkhu*=cakshus, 'eye;' *gavakkha*, 'bull's eye,' but *gavacchita*, Jât. i. 60; *rukkha* and *vaccha*=vṛiksha, 'a tree,' Mil. 209, Suttavibh. i. 179; *khudda*=kshudra, 'small' (*chudda*, 'mean,' is not the same word, but participle to the root *chubh*=kshiv, Trenckner, Mil. 130), *khamâ* = kshamâ, 'patience' and 'earth;' in the latter signification also *chamâ*, comp. Hem. ii. 18; *akkocchi*=akrukshît √kruç, Kacc. 13. Sometimes the aspiration is dropped, as in *Takkasilâ* = Takshaçilâ, 'a city in the Punjab;' *ikka* = ṛiksha, 'a bear' (also written *isa* and *issa* in Abhidhânapp.), *Okkâka* = Ikshvâku. *Patissâ*, 'obedience,' is = pratîkshâ according to Senart Mahâvastu 516; *appatissavâsa* occurs Jât. ii. 352.

Ts and *ps* generally become *cch*, as in *jighacchâ* = jighatsâ, 'hunger;' *châta*, 'hungry, desirous,' and its opposite *nicchâta*, Fausb. S. N. 143, from psâ, *saṃvacchara* (and *vacchara*, Saddhammop. v. 239) = saṃvatsara, 'year;' *bîbhacca*=bîbhatsa, 'loathsome;' and from the same root *nibbhaccheti*, 'to rebuke,' Jât. ii. 338. Exceptions are most of the roots beginning with *s* when composed with the preposition *ut*, which gives the group *ss*, as *ussada*=utsada, 'desire,' Fausb. S. N. 149, generally used in the compound *ussadaniraya*, where Burnouf translates it 'protuberance,' comp. Mahâvastu 372; and the verb *ussâdiyati*, 'to be spoiled,' C. vi. 11, 3, Suttavibh. ii. 99. We find, however, also the regular form *ucchadeṭi*, Mil. 241; *ucchâdana*, 'rubbing the body with perfumes,' Gr. 10, Mil. 315; *ucchaṅga* = utsaṅga, 'the hip.'

Çc becomes *cch*, as in *niccharati*=niçcar, 'to proceed.' An exception is *niccitta* (for *niccita*, corr.), 'thoughtless,' Dh. 173, Jât. ii. 298.

Shk and *ṣk* generally become *kkh*, as *nikkha* or *nekkha* = nishka, 'golden ornament.' Exceptions are most of the roots beginning with *k* when composed with the preposition *nis*, which in Saṃskṛit must result in *shk*, but in Pâli only gives *kk*, e. g., *nikkaḍḍhati*, 'to expel,'=nishkṛish; we have, however, the group *kkh* in *nekkhamma* = naishkâmya, 'abandonment of desires,' Vinaya texts, i. 104; and in *nikkhamati* = nishkram, 'to depart' (*nikkam* only Mil. 245, Kh. 8); *takkara*=taskara, 'a thief;' *avakkâra* = avaskâra in *avakkârapâtî*, 'slop-basin,' M. iv. 1, 2.

Sht and *shth* become *ṭṭh* in *bhaṭṭha*=bhrashṭa, 'fallen' and =bhṛishṭa, 'fried;' *paṭṭhu* = prashṭha, 'clever' (Buddhagh. *cheka*, *samattha*) Suttavibh. i. 210, ii. 60, 254, *maṭṭha* and *maṭṭa* = mṛishṭa, 'polished;' *vaṭṭa* = vṛishṭa, from *vassati*, 'to rain' (*vuṭṭha*, Jât. iii. 484); *aṭṭaka*=ashṭaka (Buddh. *aḍḍhaka*), Suttavibh. i. 81; *leḍḍu*=leshṭu, 'a clod of earth.'

St and *sth* generally become *tth*, as in *adhivattha*=adhivasta, 'living on' (*adhivuttha*, Mahâparin. 23), *parivattha*, and *pari-*

vuttha; *apattha*=apâsta, 'thrown away,' Dh. 27; *pattha*=prastha, 'a measure of capacity;' *aṭṭhi*=asthi, 'bone.' *Tt* in *niratta*=nirasta, 'rejected,' Fausb. S. N. 150; *hîyattana*=hyastana, 'yesterday's;' *bhaddamutta*=bhadramusta, 'Cyperus rotundus,' M. vi. 3, 1; *nettiṃsa*=nistriṃça, 'merciless,' Jât. ii. 77; *urattâliṃ*=urastâḍam, 'beating the breast,' Mil. 11. *St* remains in *viddhasta*=vidhvasta, 'broken;' it becomes *ss* in *vassa*=basta, 'goat,' but also *bhasta*, Jât. iii. 278.

Shp and *sp* generally become *pph*, as in *puppha*=pushpa, 'a flower;' *nipphala*=nishphala, 'fruitless;' *pp* in *bappa* or *vappa*=bâshpa, 'a tear,' M. x. 2, 13; *vanappati* = vanaspati, 'a tree,' *duppûra* = dushpûra, 'difficult to fill,' Dh. 392; *nippâpa* = nishpâpa, 'sinless,' Dh. 37; *poṭṭhabba* for *phoṭṭhabba*, 'contact,' Jât. ii. 81; *appoṭheti* = âsphoṭayati, 'to snap the fingers.'

Groups of nasals with sibilants can either be assimilated or remain unchanged, or insert a vowel between the nasal and the sibilant, or change the sibilant to *h* with metathesis.

Çn and *sn*: *pañha* = praçna, 'question,' and *paripañhati*, 'to consider,' *sinâna* and *nahâna*=snâna, 'bathing;' for *sinâni*, 'powder' Assalâyanasutta 13 comp. *snânîya* = cûrṇa, Pânini 3, 3, 113 schol.

Shn: *uṇha* = ushṇa, 'hot,' but *sîtunnaka* for *sîtuṇhaka*, M. viii. 10, 2; *taṇhâ* and *tasiṇâ*=tṛishṇâ, 'thirst;' *osaṇhati*, C. v. 2, 3, is a derivative from *saṇha* = çlakshṇa, 'smooth.'

Çm, *shm*, *sm*: *sita*, *mihita*=smita, 'smile;' *massu*=çmaçru, 'beard;' *gimha* = grîshma, 'summer;' *asman*=açman, 'stone,' but *amhanâ*, Fausb. S. N. 71; *amhe* = asme, 'us,' but *asme*, Jât. iii. 359; *usmâ* = ushman, 'heat,' Mil. 153; *bhasma* and *bhesma* = bhîsma, C. vii. 4, 8, Ab. 167; *raṃsi* and *rasmi*=raçmi, 'beam;' *pamussati*, 'to forget,' is derived by S. Goldschmidt, K.Z. xxv. 437, from a root smṛish, to which also belongs Prâk. pambusaï, pambuṭṭha, Hem. iv. 75, 184, 258; and this derivation seems to be confirmed by the spelling *pammuṭṭha* and *pammussitvâ*, Dh. 247, 248, Jât. iii. 511.

The groups *hṇ, hm,* generally show metathesis, as *gaṇhâti* = gṛihṇâti, 'to take;' *jimha* = jihma, 'crooked,' spelt *jima*, Jât. i. 290; *hn* becomes *nt* in *majjhantika* for majjhahnika, 'midday.'

The rules of the changes of three or more consonants are, on the whole, the same as those concerning two consonants which have just been laid down. When assimilation takes place an explosive prevails over the other consonants; *sattha* = çastra, 'a weapon,' but fem. *sattî* = çastrî, 'a knife;' *uddha* and *ubbha* = ûrdhva, 'high;' *tikkhiṇa*, *tikka* and *tiṇha* = tîkshṇa, 'sharp;' *kasiṇa* = kṛitsna, 'entire,' but *subhakiṇha* or °*kiṇṇa* = çubha-kṛitsna; *dosina* and *junhâ* = jyotsna, jyotsnâ, 'a moon-lit night;' *anupakhajja* = anupraskandja, 'having occupied;' *uplâvita* = utplâvita, 'floated,' Mah. 230; *bhastâ* = bhastrâ, 'bellows,' is only known from Abhidhânapp.

Rdr is changed to *ll* in *alla* = ârdra, 'wet,' Prâk. alla, olla or ulla, Hem. i. 82, but we find also *adda*, Jât. i. 244, and *addâ* = ârdrâ, 'name of a Nakshatra,' Ab. 58, *addaka* = ârdraka, 'green ginger,' Ab. 459; *rdhr* becomes *ddh* in *vaddha* = vardhra, 'leather,' Jât. ii. 154, Ang. p. 110.

Tty and *ttr*, where they are not assimilated, are simplified into *ty* and *tr* or *tt*, as in *ratyâ* instr. of *ratti* = râtri, 'night;' *vimuttâyatana* = vimukti + âyatana, 'point of emancipation;' *utrâsa* and *utrasta*, or *uttâsa* and *uttasta* = uttrâsa, uttrasta, *satra* = sattra, 'sacrifice;' *udriyati*, M. iii. 8, 1, Suttavibh. i. 254, stands for uddriyati, 'to split open,' and the substantive *udrîyanaṃ* occurs Jât. i. 72.

§ 13. Rules on Sandhi.

The rules on sandhi in Pâli may be divided into rules on vowel-sandhi, and rules on mixed sandhi where a vowel and a consonant are concerned. Consonantal sandhi does not occur in Pâli. All the rules we are about to give only deal with the so-called external sandhi, as the rules on internal sandi form a part of the phonetics we have given above. We only speak here about the sandhi of words, the sandhi of compounds belonging to the chapter on the formation of the stem.

Word-sandhi is not imperative in Pâli as in Saṃskṛit; it only takes place in certain cases, and the MSS. vary greatly as to its use or neglect. In prose it is almost confined to indeclinables and pronouns, in juxta-position or in connection with a verb or a noun, as e.g., *my ayaṃ* = me ayaṃ, *yan nûna* = yad nûna, *tasseva* = tassa eva, *tatth Ânanda*, etc. The particles that are almost regularly found in sandhi are *ca, iti* (*ti*), *api* (*pi*), *eva*, as *kathañ ca* = kathaṃ ca, *kiñcid eva* = kiñci eva, *tathâpi* = tathâ api, etc. The negative *na*, followed by a vowel, generally loses its *a*, as *n'atthi, n'eva, nâhosi*, which Trenckner, Pâli Misc. 81, prefers writing *na tthi*, as though the root *as* had lost its initial *a*. So he also writes *tâva 'ham, eva 'ham*, Mil. 219; *tattha 'ham* and *nâma 'haṃ*, and the same with *ayaṃ*, although *nâmâhaṃ* and *nâmâyaṃ* are equally frequent.

The other cases of word-sandhi in prose, without any indeclinable or pronoun, are divided by Childers into three categories: (1) a vocative beginning with a vowel is preceded by a word ending in a vowel, as *gacch' âvuso, pañcah' Upâli, âyâm' Ânanda;* (2) a verb is preceded or followed by a noun in grammatical relation with it, as *utthâyâsanâ*, *âsanâ vuṭṭhâya*, *upajjhâyass' ârocesuṃ*; (3) two nouns are in grammatical relation, as *dukkhass' antaṃ*, *dvîh' âkârehi.*

In verse word-sandhi is much more frequent than in prose, under the influence of metrical exigency; in later texts, like Dîpavaṃsa, Mahâvaṃsa, Buddhavaṃsa, Cariyâpiṭaka, and especially Khuddasikkhâ, it is not uncommon that whole syllables disappear in a sandhi where it is required by the metre, as e.g. *chaṅgula* = *chaḍaṅgula*, Mah. 211; *dasahassî* = *dasasahassî*, Bv. xiii. 21; *ticattârîsahassâni*, Bv. xvi. 15.

I. *Vowel Sandhi.*

A + *a*, *â* followed by a single consonant gives *â*, as *nâhosi* = *na* + *ahosi*, *nâsakkhi* = *na* + *asakkhi*; if a double consonant follows the *a* remains short, and an apostrophe is put generally after the terminating consonant of the first word, to show that a vowel has been dropped, as in *n' atthi* = *na atthi*, *pan' aññaṃ* = *pana aññaṃ*. In a few instances we find a long *â* before a double consonant, as *nâssa* = *na assa*, Dh. 23, comp. above the chapter on the quantity of vowels, p. 13. A short *a* before a single consonant occurs also in a few instances, as *c' ahaṃ*, Jât i. 3; *n' ahosi* = *na ahosi*, Dh. 155.

A or *â* + *i* or *î* gives *e*, as in Skt., e.g. *kokilâyeva* = *kokilâya* + *iva*, *neresi* = *na îresi*. An exception is *iti*, which always gives *âti* with a preceding *a*, e.g. *Tissâti* = *Tissa iti*; *i* is elided by a preceding *a* in *yena 'me* = *yena ime*, *pana 'me* = *pana ime*; *â* + *i* sometimes gives *î*, as *seyyathîdaṃ* = *seyyathâ idaṃ*.

A or *â* + *u* or *û* gives *o*, as in *nopeti* = *na upeti*, *pakkhanditodadhiṃ* = *pakkhanditâ udadhiṃ*, Mah. 117. Seldom we find *û* instead, as *cûbhayaṃ* = *ca ubhayaṃ*.

A is frequently elided by *i* or *u* whether followed by a conjunct consonant or not, as in *passath' imaṃ* = *passatha imaṃ*, *yass' indriyâni* = *yassa indriyâni*.

A is generally elided before *e*, *o* : *gaṇhath' etaṃ* = *gaṇhatha etaṃ*, *iv' otataṃ* = *iva otataṃ*.

Â sometimes elides a following *i*, *u* or *e* in *eva* : *disvâ' panissayam*=*disvâ upanissayaṃ*, *sutvâ' va* = *sutvâ eva*, Das. 4. Generally *â* is elided before a long vowel or before a short vowel followed by a conjunct consonant : *tath' eva* = *tathâ eva*, *tay' ajja* = *tayâ ajja*, seldom before a short vowel followed by a single consonant ; *muñcitv' ahaṃ* = *muñcitvâ ahaṃ* ; Jât. i. 13.

I is generally elided before short or long vowels, as *gacchâm' ahaṃ* = *gachâmi ahaṃ*, *idân' ime* = *idâni ime*, *dasah' upâgata*= *dasahi upâgata*, *dvîh' âkârehi* = *dvîhi âkârehi*, etc. Sometimes it remains and elides the following vowel : *phalanti 'saniyo*= *phalanti asaniyo*, *idâni 'ssa* = *idani assa* ; *i*+*a* occasionally gives *â* : *kiñcâpi* = *kiñci api*, *pâhaṃ* = *pi ahaṃ*.

Î is seldom elided : *tuṇh' assa*=*tuṇhî assa* ; at Jât. iii. 414, we have *dassâhaṃ* = *dâsî*+*ahaṃ*.

I+*i* gives *î* : *palujjîti*=*palujji iti*, Par. 40. *I* preceded by *t* (*tt*) and followed by another vowel may become *y* : *jîvanty elaka* =*jîvanti elaka*, *guty atha* = *gutti atha*. Generally, however, the group *ty* is changed to *cc*, especially when the first word is *iti* : *iccevaṃ* = *ity evaṃ*. The corresponding change of *dy* to *jj* is not attested by any good authority. *Api* followed by a vowel may become *app* through an intermediate *apy* : *app eva* =*api eva* ; *itv*, *tv* for *iti*, *ti* is most probably only a corrupt spelling.

U is elided before a vowel : *samet' âyasmâ* = *sametu âyasmâ*, *tâs' eva* = *tâsu eva*. Rarely it elides a following vowel : *nu' ttha*=*nu attha*, *kinnu' mâ*=*kinnu imâ*. *U*+*i* sometimes gives *û* : *sâdhûti* = *sâdhu* + *iti*. Before *a* or *e* it can be changed to *v* : *vatthv ettha* = *vatthu ettha*, *sesesv ayaṃ* = *sesesu ayaṃ*.

E may be elided before a long vowel or before a short vowel followed by a conjunct consonant: *m' âsi* = *me âsi*, *sac' assa* = *sace assa*; sometimes it elides a following vowel: *te' me* = *te ime*, *sace' jja* = *sace ajja*, *re' yya* = *re ayya*, Mil. 124; occasionally *e* + *a* gives *â*, as *sacâyaṃ* = *sace* + *ayaṃ*, Dh. 140, 165; but the *e* can also be turned into *y*, as if it were *i*, and an *a* following lengthened by compensation when a single consonant follows: *tyâhaṃ* = *te ahaṃ*, *myâyaṃ* = *me ayaṃ*, *ty ajja* = *te ajja*; exception, *tyâssa* = *te assa*.

O is elided before a long vowel or a short vowel followed by a double consonant: *kut' ettha* = *kuto ettha*, *tay' assu* = *tayo assu*, *tat' uddhaṃ* = *tato uddhaṃ*. It elides a following vowel in *so'haṃ* = *so ahaṃ*, *cattâro' me* = *cattâro ime*, etc. *O* + *a* gives *â*: *dukkhâyaṃ* = *dukkho ayaṃ*, Jât. i. 168. *O* can also be turned into *v* (as *e* into *y*) and an initial *a* lengthened if followed by a single consonant: *yvâhaṃ* = *yo ahaṃ*, *khvassa* = *kho assa*, *yveva* = *yo eva*: exceptions, *svâssu* = *so assu*, Jât. i. 196; *khvâssa* = *kho assa*, Payoga Siddhi.

Euphonic consonants are often inserted when two vowels meet, to avoid a hiatus; especially the semi-vowels *y* and *v* are used for this purpose.

Y is inserted between a word terminating in *a* or *â*, when followed by *idaṃ* or any of the oblique cases of this pronoun which begins with *i*: *na yidaṃ* = *na idaṃ*, *mâ yime* = *mâ ime*, *yathayidaṃ* = *yathâ idaṃ* with shortening of the *â*. The same process takes place with *eva* and *iva*, which latter, however, is changed to *viya* by metathesis. When *a*, *â* is followed by *u*, *û*, *v* may be inserted for euphony: *bhantâ vudikkhati* = *bhantâ udikkhati*.

Sometimes a euphonic *m* is inserted between two vowels: *idha-m-âhu* = *idha âhu*, *pariganiya-m-asesam* = *pariganiya asesam*, Girimânandasutta in Paritta, *kapi-m-âgantvâ*, Cariy. ii. 5, 4; or *r* if the following word is *iva*: *âragge-r-iva* = *âragge iva*, *sâsapo-r-iva* = *sâsapo iva*, *sikhâ-r-iva* = *sikhâ iva*, Mahâsamayas. 21. Final *â* is shortened before this *r* in *yatha-r-iva*, *tatha-r-iva* = *yathâ eva*, *tathâ eva*, Kacc. 19.

In a great many cases a lost consonant is revived to avoid the hiatus, as in *yasmâd apeti* = yasmâd apeti, *kocid eva* = kaçcid eva, *tunhîm âsina* = tûshṇîm âsîna, *vuttir esâ* = vṛittir eshâ, *chaḷabhiññâ* = shaḍabhijñâ, *puthag eva* = pṛithag eva, *pag eva* = prâg eva, with shortening of the *â*, *sammadaññâ* = samyag âjñâ, with change of *g* to *d*, and *anvad* = anvak in a passage of the Maggasaṃyutta quoted by Morris, 'Report on Pâli literature,' p. 5. *Dhir atthu*, Jât. i. 59, stands for *dhig atthu*, *vijjur eva* for *vijjud eva*. Jât. iii. 464 we have *jîvar eva* for *jîvann eva*; *attadatha* stands for *attanattha* = âtman + artha, *satthud anvaya* for *satthur anvaya*, *punad eva* for *punar eva*.

II. *Mixed Sandhi.*

Original double consonants simplified by assimilation at the beginning of a word, can again be doubled after a word terminating in a vowel: *yatra tthitaṃ* = *yatra thitaṃ* for yatra sthitam. This is often done in verse when a long syllable is required.

In a few cases a lost final consonant is revived before a consonant, as *yâvañ c' idaṃ* = *yâva ca idaṃ*, *suhanus sahâ*, Jât. ii. 31, *tayas su* = *trayas svid*, Kh. 9.

As we have seen above, p. 45, sometimes anusvâra stands for an original consonant, and in this case before a vowel it is liable to be replaced by the original consonant. Sakṛit becomes *sakiṃ* in Pâli, but before a vowel we have *sakid*; in the same way we have *tad* for *taṃ*, *yad* for *yaṃ*, etc.

In verse when a short syllable is required, anusvâra can be elided before a consonant: *no ce muñceyya candimaṃ* for *muñceyyaṃ* Candaparitta, *âkaṅkha virâgaṃ* for *âkaṅkhaṃ*, Dh. v. 343. Or else the whole syllable may be dropped, as in *rajovajall' ukkuṭikappamâṇaṃ* as the metre requires, Dh. v. 141; *piyân' adassanaṃ* for *piyânaṃ*, Dh. v. 210; *pâpân' akaraṇaṃ*, for *pâpânaṃ*, v. 333; *nipajj' ahaṃ* for *nipajjiṃ*, Jât. i. 13. When the anusvâra is dropped the remaining *a* can be contracted with a following *a* to *â*, as in *saccâhaṃ*=*satyaṃ ahaṃ*, Suttavibh. i. 190; *labheyyâhaṃ*=*labheyyaṃ ahaṃ*, Parin. 59; *idâhaṃ*=*idaṃ*+*ahaṃ* in the phrase *ekam idâhaṃ samayaṃ*, comp. Oldenberg, K.Z. xxv. 325.

Only in late texts an anusvâra can elide a following vowel, as *cirassaṃ' dhunâ* for *adhunâ*, *vassantaṃ 'malakam* in two passages from Pâli Burmese books quoted by Oldenberg, 'India Office Catalogue, p. 121,' *sovaṇṇamayaṃ 'nuññâtaṃ* for *anuññâtaṃ*, Khuddasikkhâ, xxxvi. 15.

§ 14. Declension.

We distinguish in Pâli, as in Saṃskṛit, stems ending in vowels and stems ending in consonants, and according to this division the whole declension of substantives and adjectives is arranged. It must however be remarked, that the vowel stems have largely encroached upon the consonantal stems, and that only fragments of a consonantal inflexion have remained. Especially consonantal stems identical with roots, which are frequent enough in Saṃskṛit, have almost totally disappeared from Pâli, and have been replaced by dissyllabic stems increased by the addition of a vowel. A careful investigation of the old texts has only yielded the following instances of consonantal root-stems: *taco*, pl. of tvac, 'skin,' Dh. 111, Kh. 3; *pâdâ*, instr. of pad, 'foot,' Dh. 164; *vâcâ*, instr. of vâc, 'speech,' Kh. 9; *pamudi*, loc. of pramud, 'joy,' Gr. 139; *parisati* and *parisatiṃ*, Suttavibh. ii. 285, loc. of parishad, 'assembly.'

There are two possibilities of turning these consonantal stems into vowel-stems: (1) The terminating consonant is dropped, and the word passes into the declension of that vowel which now stands at the end, e.g. *upanisâ*=upanishad; *âpâ*= âpad, Jât. ii. 317, which are inflected like feminine *â*-stems; *âsi* = âçis, 'blessing,' inflected like an *i*-stem; *maru* = marut, name of a 'deva,' inflected like an *u*-stem. (2) The stem is increased by the addition of an *a* (which may represent originally the termination of the acc. sing., comp. however Pischel, Beitr. iii. 262), and the word is now inflected like an *a*-stem, masculine, feminine or neuter, according to the gender of the original noun. Such instances are *kita* = kṛit, and *visagata* for *visakata*=vishakṛit, Suttavibh. i. 80; *tivutâ*=trivṛit, name of a 'plant;' *barihisa*=barhis, 'sacrificial grass.' Sometimes the gender is changed, as in *sarado* m. 'year'= çarad f. comp. Pischel gramm. Prâc. 5; Beitr. iii. 240. Change of gender is very frequent in Pâli, as for instance in *vacîbheda*, Khuddasikkhâ xl. 1, we have instead of *â* the thematic vowel *î*, and as this is also found in some other compounds, I do not believe that *vaci* is a locative like tvaci in tvacisâra, Pâṇ. vi. 3, 9; comp. Jainaprâk. vatîjoa Beitr. 5. *Âp* is generally used in the nom. pl. *âpo*, we find however a gen. *âpassa*, Mil. 363.

Only very few vestiges of the dual occur in the texts known to us at present: *to idh' âgato*, 'these two having come,' Dîp. 56; *ubho* = ubhau, Dh. v. 74, 306; *mâtâpitu*, 'father and mother,' Cariy. ii. 9, 7, if this does not stand for the acc.

°pitṛîn. Generally the plural replaces the dual even in such cases as *jayampatî* and *tudampatî*, 'man and wife,' where the meaning clearly points to a duality.

I. *Vowel Bases.*

Masculine and Neuter in *a*.

Dhamma, 'The Law.'

	Singular.	Plural.
Nom.	*dhammo.*	*dhammâ, dhammâse.*
Voc.	*dhamma, dhammâ.*	*dhammâ.*
Acc.	*dhammaṃ.*	*dhamme.*
Instr.	*dhammena.*	*dhammebhi, dhammehi.*
Dat.	*dhammassa (dhammâya).*	*dhammânaṃ.*
Abl.	*dhammâ, dhammasmâ, dhammamhâ.*	*dhammebhi, dhammehi.*
Gen.	*dhammassa.*	*dhammânaṃ.*
Loc.	*dhamme, dhammasmiṃ, dhammamhi.*	*dhammesu.*

Rûpa, 'The Image.'

	Singular.	Plural.
Nom. }	*rûpaṃ.*	
Voc. }	*rûpaṃ.*	*rûpâni, rûpâ.*
Acc. }	*rûpaṃ.*	*rûpâni, rûpe.*
Instr.	*rûpena.*	*rûpebhi, rûpehi.*
Dat	*rûpassa (rûpâya).*	*rûpânaṃ.*
Abl.	*rûpâ, rûpasmâ, rûpamhâ.*	*rûpebhi, rûpehi.*
Gen.	*rûpassa.*	*rûpânaṃ.*
Loc.	*rûpe, rûpasmiṃ, rûpamhi.*	*rûpesu.*

The form given in the table as *dative* is, properly speaking, the genitive = Skt. dharmasya, rûpasya, which has taken up the functions of dative in Pâli. The old dative in *âya*, which I have given in paranthesis, is only used to denote the intention, and is almost synonymous with an infinitive; only few instances occur where the dative has a terminative meaning as Dh. v. 174, *saggâya gacchati*, 'goes to heaven,' and Dh. v. 311, *nirayâya upakaḍḍhati*, 'brings to hell,' comp. Pischels remarks, Beitr. zur kunde d. indog. Spr. i. 111, 119; *lokânukampâya* = *lokam anukampituṃ*, 'through compassion for the world;' *na patthaye nirayaṃ dassanâya*, 'I do not wish to see the hell.' Especially the dative *atthâya* is used frequently with the meaning 'for the good of, for the sake of,' as in *Buddhassa atthâya jîvitam pariccajâmi*, 'for Buddha's sake I will lay down my life,' comp. Childers, s. v. We have also an abridged form *atthâ* used in the same sense, e.g. in *bhojanatthâ*, 'for the sake of food,' Jât iii. 425. Other instances of this abridged dative are *esanâ* = *esanâya*, 'in search of,' Ten Jât. 48, 81; *anâpucchâ* = anâpucchâya, 'without asking leave,' comp. *paripucchâya*, Mil. 93; *lâbhâ* in such sentences as *lâbhâ vata no*, 'this is for our advantage,' which Childers explained as a dative, is in reality a nom. fem. identical with the masc. *lâbha*, comp. Senart Mahâvastu 550.

The ablative stands for the instrumental in *javâ*, 'speedily,' Dîp. 23; and *ahiṃsâ*, 'through pity,' Dh. v. 270. The suffix *sâ* is very often also used to denote an instr., as in *vâhasâ*, 'by dint of,' Mil. 379; Suttavibh. ii. 158 (comp. the v. l.); *talasâ*, 'by the sole of the foot' (com. *pâdatalena*), Jât. ii. 223; *rasasâ*, 'by taste,' Jât. iii. 328; *bilasâ*, *padasâ*, Kacc. 91; *balasâ*, 'by force,' Cariy. ii. 4, 7.

In the ablative the terminations in *dhammasmâ*, *dham-*

mamhâ, and in the loc., *dhammasmiṃ*, *dhammamhi*, are taken from the pronominal inflection. Besides, we have two other terminations for the ablative, *to* = skt. tas, and *so* = ças, which occur mostly in later texts, but also in a few instances in the Jâtaka and Dhp. Instances are *gaṇanâto*, 'by number,' Jât. i. 29; *câpâto*, 'from the bow,' Dh. v. 320; *devato*, 'from a deva,' Bv. xvi. 7; *orato pâraṃ gacchati*, *pârato oram âgacchati* 'goes from this end of the field to the further end and back again from the far end to this,' Jât. i. 57; *mettâto*, 'from friendship,' Saddhammop. v. 487, 489. With *so* we have *bhâgaso*, 'by portion,' Mil. 330; *parivattaso*, 'by turns,' Mahâparin. 60; *tîṇi yojanaso*, 'three yojanas wide,' Bv. xxi. 24.

In the locative the forms in *e* and in *smim* or *mhi* are almost equally frequent already in earlier texts, see Torp, Die Flexion des Pâli, p. 18. The forms *bilasi* and *padasi* given by Kacc. 91 do not occur anywhere else. The locative is used instead of a dative in *brâhmaṇe*, Cariy. i. 9, 47.

In the nom. pl. of the masculine we have a form in *âse* which corresponds to the vedic nom. pl. in *âsas*, as *paṇḍitâse*, 'the learned,' Fausb. S. N. xi. 167; *rukkhâse*, 'the trees,' Jât. iii. 399, comp. Oldenberg, KZ. xxv. 315.

The acc. pl. of the masculines in *e* is somewhat difficult to explain: Kuhn compares it to the vedic pronominal forms *asme*, *yushme*, which are used likewise for the nominative and accusative, and refers to the explanation offered by Schleicher, Compendium p. 611 for these forms; comp. Torp p. 19, S. Goldschmidt, KZ. xxv. 438.

The instr. pl. in *ebhi* or *ehi* quite corresponds to the vedic form in *ebhis* (or to the ablative in *ebhyas*, as the forms are the same in Pâli). Instances for the form in *bhi* are given by Oldenberg, KZ. xxv. 316, 317. In old texts we find besides a form in *e* corresponding to the instr. of the classical Saṃskrit in *ais*, for inst. *vanîpake*, used as a dative, 'to the beggars,' Cariy. i. 4, 9; *yâcake*, ib. i. 8, 12; *adhane âture jiṇṇe yâcake paṭṭhike jane samaṇabrahmaṇe khîṇe deti dânaṃ akiñcane*, ib. i. 1, 9; *guṇe dasah' upâgataṃ*, instr., Jât. i. 6.

In the plural of the neuter we have the regular form *cittâni* for nom. and acc., and besides *rûpâ* for the nom., and *rûpe* for the acc., which are both taken from the masculine declension. Thus we have *satte dukkhâ pamocayi*, 'he released the beings from pain,' Mah. 2; *pâṇe vihiṃsati*, v. l. for *pâṇâni hiṃsati*, 'he hurts living creatures,' Vasala sutta v. 2. The same confusion of gender occurs in *pabbatâni*, Dh. v. 188 (probably through attraction from *vanâni*), in *dukkhâ*, 'sorrow,' which may be used as neuter and masc., and (according to Fausböll), even as fem.

In the locative pl. Childers gives a form *milakkhusu* from *milakkha*, 'a barbarian,' but without any reference.

Feminine in *â*.

Kaññâ, 'The Girl.'

	Singular.	Plural.
Nom.	*kaññâ.*	*kaññâ, kaññâyo.*
Voc.	*kaññe.*	*kaññâ, kaññâyo.*
Acc.	*kaññaṃ.*	*kaññâ, kaññâyo.*
Instr.	*kaññâya.*	*kaññâbhi, kaññâhi.*
Dat.	*kaññâya.*	*kaññânaṃ.*
Abl.	*kaññâya.*	*kaññâbhi, kaññâhi.*
Gen.	*kaññâya.*	*kaññânaṃ.*
Loc.	*kaññâyaṃ, kaññâya.*	*kaññâsu.*

In the vocative we have the following exceptions: *ammâ*,

annâ, *ambâ*, *tâtâ*, all signifying 'mother,' form the voc. like the nom., Kacc. p. 64; of *ammâ*, we have besides a voc. *amma*, frequent in Dh. The loc. *kaññâya* is taken from the genitive. For the nom. pl. in *â* and *âyo*, comp. Oldenberg, Kz. xxv. 317.

Masculine and Neuter in *i*.

Aggi, 'The Fire.'

	Singular.	Plural.
N. & V.	*aggi.*	*aggayo, aggî.*
Acc.	*aggiṃ.*	*aggî, aggayo.*
Instr.	*agginâ.*	*aggîbhi, aggîhi.*
Dat.	*aggino, aggissa.*	*aggînaṃ.*
Abl.	*agginâ, aggismâ, aggimhâ.*	*aggîbhi, aggîhi.*
Gen.	*aggino, aggissa.*	*aggînaṃ.*
Loc.	*aggismiṃ, aggimhi.*	*aggîsu.*

Akkhi, 'The Eye.'

	Singular.	Plural.
N. & V.	*akkhi, akkiṃ.*	*akkhîni, akkhî.*
Acc.	*akkiṃ.*	*akkhîni, akkhî.*
Instr.	*akkhinâ.*	*akkhîbhi, akkhîhi.*
Dat.	*akkhino, akkhissa.*	*akkhînaṃ.*
Abl.	*akkhinâ, akkhismâ, akkhimhâ.*	*akkhîbhi, akkhîhi.*
Gen.	*akkhino, akkhissa.*	*akkhînaṃ.*
Loc.	*akkhismiṃ, akkhimhi.*	*akkhîsu.*

A voc. *ise*, corresponding to the Skt. ṛishe, occurs in Rûpasiddhi, and Jât. xix. 1, 2. A gen. *mune*, is given by Oldenberg, KZ. xxv. 318. The ancient loc. in *o*, is only formed from the stem *âdi*, according to Kacc. 41, *âdo* and *âdu*, Dh. 96;

a loc. *gire*, after the analogy of the *a*-stems, occurs Jât. iii. 157. An instr. after the same analogy is *buddharaṃsena*, Bv. x. 28. Besides, we very often, especially in Dîp., find the simple stem used for almost any case of the sing., see Oldenberg, KZ. xxv. 318.

A nom. pl. *aggino*, is found Saddhammop. v. 586, together with the regular form *aggayo*. In the oblique cases of the plural we only find the short *i* occasionally in verses, as *ñâtihi*, *paṭisanthâravuttinaṃ*, Dh. 146.

Instances of the nominative accusative of neuters in *ṃ*, formed after the analogy of the *a*-stems are not very frequent, but numerous enough to show that the form really exists: *akkhiṃ*, Dh. 140; *aṭṭhiṃ*, Das. J. 5, 12. The nominative plural *akkhî*, occurs Dh. 82.

Feminine in ĭ.

Ratti, 'The Night.'

	Singular.	Plural.
N. Voc.	*ratti.*	*rattiyo, rattî.*
Acc.	*rattiṃ.*	*rattî, rattiyo.*
Ins. Abl.	*rattiyâ.*	*rattîbhi, rattîhi.*
D. Gen.	*rattiyâ.*	*rattînaṃ.*
Loc.	*rattiyaṃ, rattiyâ.*	*rattîsu.*

The nominative plural *rattî*, is formed exactly like the corresponding form of the masculine stems *aggî*, most probably after the analogy of the *a*-stems (Torp. 41). In the genitive sing. we have a form *kasino* like *aggino* in Kasibhâradvâjasutta v. 1, and in the locative *ratto* = *âdo*, Dh. v. 299. The locative singular in *â*, is properly speaking a genitive, as we have noticed also in *kaññâ* confusion between these two cases. Instead of the group *iy* in the oblique cases of the singular, and in the nominative accusative of the plural, we also find simple *y*, and this may be contracted with a preceding dental according to the rules given above, p. 49. In this way we obtain forms like *nikatyâ*, from nikṛiti, 'fraud,' Jât. ii. 183, *nikacca* with shortened *â*, Suttavibh. i. 90; *jaccâ* for *jâtiyâ*; *sammuccâ* for *sammutiyâ*, etc., comp. Fausb., introd. to the Suttanipâta transl. p. xi. Instead of *rattiyâ* we have *ratyâ*, Dh. 178.

The declension of the stems in *î* is very much the same as of those in *ĭ*:

Nadî, 'A River.'

	Singular.	Plural.
N. Voc.	*nadî.*	*nadiyo*, *najjo*, *nadî.*
Acc.	*nadiṃ.*	*nadî*, *nadiyo*, *najje*
Ins. Abl.	*nadiyâ*, *nadyâ*, *najjâ.*	*nadîbhi*, *nadîhi.*
D. Gen.	*nadiyâ*, *nadyâ*, *najjâ.*	*nadînaṃ.*
Loc.	*nadiyaṃ*, *najjaṃ*, *nadiyâ.*	*nadîsu.*

In the ablative singular we have a contracted form *pesî* for *pesiyâ*, Mil. 421, an ablative in *to* is *sirito* from *sirî* = çrî, Samanta Pâs. 304. From *dabbî*, 'spoon,' we have the genitive *davyâ*, Jât. iii. 218. The nominative plural *najjo* occurs only Kacc. 56. An enlarged form of the genitive plural in *iyânaṃ*, is met with in a few examples: *bhaginîyânaṃ*, Mah. 4; *tevîsatiyânaṃ*, Dh. 117; *caturasîtiyânaṃ*, Dh. 350; it supposes a nominative singular in *iyâ*, like çriyâ for çrî in the Saṃskrit of the Northern Bhuddhists.

The declension of *itthî* or *thî* = strî, 'a woman,' follows *nadî* in general; in the acc. singular we have an additional form *itthiyaṃ* = striyaṃ, in the genitive *thiyaṃ* = stryâm, in the locative *itthiyâ*.

Masculines and Neuters in *u*.

Bhikkhu, 'A Mendicant Friar.'

	Singular.	Plural.
Nom.	*bhikkhu.*	*bhikkhavo, bhikkhû.*
Voc.	*bhikkhu.*	*bhikkhavo, bhikkhave, bhikkhû.*
Acc.	*bhikkhuṃ.*	*bhikkhû, bhikkhavo.*
Instr.	*bhikkhunâ.*	*bhikkhûbhi, bhikkhûhi.*
D. G.	*bhikkhuno, bhikkhussa.*	*bhikkhûnaṃ.*
Abl.	*bhikkhunâ, bhikkhusmâ, bhikkhumhâ.*	*bhikkhûbhi, bhikkhûhi.*
Loc.	*bhikkhusmiṃ, bhikkhumhi.*	*bhikkhûsu.*

In the voc. sing. we find *Sutano*, Jât. iii. 329. A rest of the old gen. in *os*, survives in *hetu* = hetos, Dh. v. 84. In the oblique cases of the plural again we find the short *u* (like the short *i*) occasionally in verses, as *jantuhi*, Anecd. 33; *bhikkhusu*, Dh. v. 73; *jantunaṃ*, Ten. Jât. 91. A form *bahunnaṃ* with double *n* instead of *û* occurs Dh. 81. Irregular forms of the nom. pl. are *jantuno* and *mittaduno* from *mittadu*=mitradrub, Mah. 10, *jantuyo* and *hetuyo*.

Masculines terminating in *û* keep it in the nom. sing., as *abhibhû*, Dh. 255, but shorten it in the other cases. The plural is *abhibhû* or *abhibhuvo*, from *sabbaññû* = sarvajñâ: *sabbaññû* or *sabbaññuno*, from *sahabhû* : *sahabhû, sahabhuvo, sahabhuno*.

The neuters in *u* form the nom. voc. acc. pl. either in *û* or *ûni*, as *madhû* or *madhûni*. The nom. and acc. sing. can take *ṃ* like the corresponding forms of the *i*-stems, as *cakkhuṃ udapâdi*, Kacc. 27.

Feminines in *ŭ*.

Dhenu, 'A Cow.'

	Singular.	Plural.
N. V.	*dhenu.*	*dhenuvo, dhenuyo, dhenû.*
Acc.	*dhenuṃ.*	*dhenû, dhenuyo.*
I. A.	*dhenuyâ.*	*dhenûbhi, dhenûhi.*
D. G.	*dhenuyâ.*	*dhenûnaṃ.*
Loc.	*dhenuyaṃ, dhenuyâ.*	*dhenûsu.*

The nom. pl. *dhenuvo* occurs Dh. 237, where Fausböll has altered it to *dhenuyo*. *Bhû*, 'the earth,' makes in the loc. sing. *bhuvi*, Kacc. 45; *massu*, though being a neuter, forms its gen. according to the fem. fashion *massuyâ*, Jât. iii. 315. An abl. with the termination *to* occurs in *natthuto*, 'into the nose,' M. viii. 1, 11, *jambuto*, Bv. xvii. 9, the loc. *dhâtuyâ*, C. ix. 1, 4.

The feminines terminating in *û* follow the declension of *dhenu* with the only exception of the nom. sing., which may adopt the form in *û* as *vadhû*, 'a wife,' Ab. 230 (but *vadhu*, Suttavibh. i. 18); *sarabhû*=sarayu, 'name of a river;' *camû* = camû, 'an army;' *pâdû* = pâdû, 'a shoe;' *sassû* = çvaçrû, 'mother-in-law.'

Stems ending in a diphthong.

Go, 'A Cow.'

	Singular.	Plural.
N. V.	*go.*	*gavo, gâvo.*
Acc.	*gavam, gâvaṃ, gâvuṃ.*	*gavo, gâvo.*
Instr.	*gavena, gâvena.*	*gobhi, gohi.*
D. G.	*gavassa, gâvassa.*	*gavaṃ, gonaṃ, gunnaṃ.*

	Singular.	Plural.
Abl.	*gavâ, gâvâ, gavasmâ, gâvasmâ, gavamhâ, gâvamhâ.*	*gobhi, gohi.*
Loc.	*gave, gâve, gavasmiṃ, gâvasmiṃ, gavamhi, gâvamhi.*	*gosu, gavesu, gâvesu.*

We find throughout the declension a new stem, *gava* or *gâva*, which is inflected like a masculine *a*-stem ; we meet even with a nom. pl. *gavâ*, Jât. i. 336, together with the nom. pl. *gâviyo*, of the fem. *gâvî*.

All other diphthongic stems have disappeared in Pâli : nau has become *nâvâ* following the declension of the feminine *â*-stems, dyu has become *divo* with the only exception of the instr. sing. *divâ*, which is used like an adverb in Pâli.

Consonantal Stems.

Stems in nasals.

These are considered by the native grammarians as belonging to the vowel-stems.

(1) in *an*.

Attan = âtman, 'Self.'

	Singular.	Plural.
Nom.	*attâ.*	*attâno.*
Voc.	*atta, attâ.*	*attâno.*
Acc.	*attânaṃ, attaṃ.*	*attâno.*
Instr.	*attanâ, [attena].*	*attanebhi, attanehi.*
D. G.	*attano.*	*attânaṃ.*
Abl.	*attanâ.*	*attanebhi, attanehi.*
Loc.	*attani.*	*attanesu.*

A parallel form is *âtumâ* with the same inflexion, and besides, *tumo*, Fausb. S. N. 170. The instr. *attena*, the abl. *attasmâ*, *attamhâ*, and the loc. *attasmiṃ*, *attamhi*, given by Clough, have not yet been found in any old text.

Brahman, 'Brahma.'

	Singular.	Plural.
Nom.	*brahmâ.*	*brahmâno.*
Voc.	*brahme.*	*brahmâno.*
Acc.	*brahmânaṃ, brahmaṃ.*	*brahmâno.*
Instr.	*brahmanâ, brahmunâ.*	*brahmebhi, brahmehi.*
D. G.	*brahmuno, [brahmassa].*	*brahmânaṃ, brahmunaṃ.*
Abl.	*brahmanâ, brahmunâ.*	*brahmebhi, brahmehi.*
Loc.	*brahmani.*	*brahmesu.*

The voc. sing. *brahme*, Kacc. 96, is formed after the analogy of the *i*-stems.

Râjan, 'A King.'

	Singular.	Plural.
Nom.	*râjâ.*	*râjâno.*
Voc.	*râja, râjâ.*	*râjâno.*
Acc.	*râjânaṃ, râjaṃ.*	*râjâno.*
Instr.	*raññâ, râjena.*	*râjûbhi, râjûhi, râjebhi, râjehi.*
D. G.	*rañño, râjino, [râjassa].*	*raññaṃ, râjûnaṃ, râjânaṃ.*
Abl.	*raññâ.*	*râjûbhi, râjûhi, râjebhi, râjehi.*
Loc.	*raññe, râjini.*	*râjûsu, râjesu.*

We find an instr. *muddhanâ* from *muddhâ*, 'the head,' Mah. 117, and a loc. *muddhani*, ib. 108; an instr. *râjaṇâ*, which

I think cannot be correct, has been given by Fausböll, Jât. iii. 180, and a gen. *raññassa*, Jât. iii. 70. The forms *râjaṃ*, *râjena* suppose a stem *râja*, *râjino* and *râjini* are simply formed by epenthesis; in the plural we have to adopt a stem *râju*, from which all the cases can be derived. The legend PAONANO PAO on the Indobactrian coins does not represent a Pâli form *râjunânaṃ râjâ* with double suffix, as Kuhn believed, but is a Skythian title formed on the model of râjâdirâjâ, comp. Oldenberg, Ind. Ant. x. 215 note.

Some substantives belonging to this declension in Saṃskṛit follow the *a*-declension in Pâli, as *Vissakammo*=Viçvakarman, 'name of a celestial architect,' spelt *Vissukamma*, Cariy i. 9, 41; *vivattachaddo*=vivṛittachadman, 'one by whom the veil is rolled away;' *puthulomo*=pṛithuloman, 'a fish;' *athabbana*=atharvan, *yakana*=yakan, 'the liver;' *chaka*, *chakana*=çakan, 'dung.'

Yuvan, 'Young.'

	Singular.	Plural.
Nom.	*yuvâ.*	*yuvâno, yuvânâ.*
Voc.	*yuva, yuvâ, yuvâna, yuvânâ.*	*yuvâno, yuvânâ.*
Acc.	*yuvânaṃ, yuvaṃ.*	*yuvâne, yuve.*
Instr.	*yuvânâ, yuvânena, yuvena.*	*yuvânebhi, yuvânehi, yuvebhi, yuvehi.*
D. G.	*yuvânassa, yuvassa.*	*yuvânânaṃ, yuvânaṃ.*
Abl.	*yuvânâ, yuvânasmâ, yuvânamhâ.*	*yuvânebhi, yuvânehi, yuvebhi, yuvehi.*
Loc.	*yuvâne, yuvânasmiṃ, yuvânamhi, yuve, yuvasmiṃ, yuvamhi.*	*yuvânesu, yuvâsu, yuvesu.*

Most of these forms suppose a new stem *yuvâna*, formed from the acc. sing. Besides we have a stem *yûna*, from which the nom. sing. *yûno*, f. *yûnî*, is formed, according to Kacc. 328.

Sâ = çvan, 'A Dog.'

	Singular.	Plural.
Nom.	*sâ.*	*sâ*, [*sâno*].
Voc.	*sa.*	*sâ.*
Acc.	*saṃ*, [*sânaṃ*].	*se.*
Instr.	*sena.*	*sâbhi*, *sâhi.*
Dat.	*sâya*, *sassa.*	*sânaṃ.*
Abl.	*sâ*, *sasmâ*, *samhâ.*	*sâbhi*, *sâhi.*
Gen.	*sassa.*	*sânaṃ.*
Loc.	*se*, *sasmiṃ*, *samhi.*	*sâsu.*

Besides we have for the nom. sing. the forms *sâno*, *svâno*, *suvâno*, *soṇo* and *sûṇo*. Other words following the same inflection are *paccakkhadhammâ* = pratyakshadharman, 'whose virtues are evident,' and *gaṇḍîvadhanvâ*, 'using the bow Gâṇḍîva,' Kacc. 182.

A few substantives form only some cases according to the nasal inflection, while the other cases follow another declension, as *kammaṃ*=karman, 'action,' which forms the instr. sing. *kammunâ*, *kammanâ* and *kammena*, the gen. *kammuno* and *kammassa*, Pât. 11; abl. *kammâ*, Dh. v. 127, loc. *kammani*. *Thâmo*=sthâmas, 'strength,' forms part of its cases after the nasal inflection as the instr. *thâmunâ*, Kacc. 81, but generally *thâmasâ*, Suttavibh. ii. 134, Mah. 143 (Turnour *thâmavâ*), gen. *thâmuno*. In the same way *addhâ*=adhvan, 'a road,' forms *addhano* and *addhuno*; *bhasmaṃ* = bhasman, 'ashes,' loc. *bhasmani*.

Pumâ=puṃs, 'a man.'

	Singular.	Plural.
Nom.	*pumâ.*	*pumâno.*
Voc.	*pumaṃ.*	*pumâno.*
Acc.	*pumaṃ.*	*pumâno.*
Instr.	*pumânâ, pumunâ, pumena.*	*pumânebhi, pumânehi.*
D. G.	*pumuno, pumassa.*	*pumânaṃ.*
Abl.	*pumunâ.*	*pumânebhi, pumânehi.*
Loc.	*pumâne, pume, pumasmiṃ, pumamhi.*	*pumâsu, pumesu.*

A nom. sing. *pumo* occurs Cariy. iii. 6, 2, similar to *tumo*= âtmâ, Fausb. S. N. 170.

(2). Adjectives terminating in *mant* and *vant.*

Guṇavant, 'virtuous.'

	Singular.	Plural.
Nom.	*guṇavâ, guṇavanto.*	*guṇavanto, guṇavantâ.*
Voc.	*guṇavaṃ, guṇava, guṇavâ.*	*guṇavanto, guṇavantâ.*
Acc.	*guṇavantaṃ, guṇavaṃ.*	*guṇavante.*
Instr.	*guṇavatâ, guṇavantena.*	*guṇavantebhi, guṇavantehi.*
D. G.	*guṇavato, guṇavantassa, guṇavassa.*	*guṇavataṃ, guṇavantânaṃ.*
Abl.	*guṇavatâ.*	*guṇavantebhi, guṇavantehi.*
Loc.	*guṇavati, guṇavante, guṇavantasmiṃ, guṇavantamhi.*	*guṇavantesu.*

The neuter has in the nom. voc. acc. sing. *guṇavaṃ*, pl. *guṇavanti, guṇavantâni.* The fem. is made by adding *î* to the strong or the weak form, *guṇavantî* or *guṇavatî;* it follows the declension of the *î*-stems.

The participles in *ant* follow this declension with the only exception of the nom. sing. which they form in *aṃ* or *anto*, as *gacchaṃ*, *gacchanto*, 'going.'

A nom. from the weak form *jîvato* for *jîvanto* occurs in a verse, Jât. iii. 539; an acc. *vajataṃ*, Vasala Sutta, v. 6; *asataṃ*, Dh. v. 73, Vasala Sutta v. 16. From the root *kar* we have the part. nom. pl. masc. *karontâ*, Dh. v. 66; nom. sing. fem. *karontî*, Dh. 246; gen. sing. masc. *karoto*, Dh. v. 116; instr. *saṃkhârontena*, in a passage of Petavatthuvaṇṇanâ quoted I. O. C. p. 79; all these forms follow the 3rd pers. pl. *karonti*. Besides we have the gen. *anukubbassa*, Jât. iii. 108, rendered in the Mahâvastu by kṛityânukâryasya.

Arahant, 'an Arhat,' forms the nom. sing. *arahaṃ* and *arahâ*, the former being the regular one, the latter following the analogy of *mahâ*. In the nom. pl. we have *arahanto* and *arahâ*, Dîp. 30, Anecd. 7. A similar nom. pl. *mahâ* occurs Ab. 413. Kacc. 94 gives a nom. sing. *mahaṃ* which does not occur anywhere else; the nom. sing. *mahâ* occurs separately, Dh. 298, Mah. 132, and besides very often in compounds.

In the pl. we have one instance of an old form *sabbhi*= sadbhis, Dh. v. 151.

In the neuter nom. sing. we have the forms *brahâ*, Ab. 700, *madhuvâ*, Dh. v. 69; *asaṃ*=asat, Jât. ii. 32.

Of participles of the perfect in vaṃs we have *bhayadassivâ*= °darçivaṃs; vidvaṃs forms nom. sing. *aviddasu*, Dh. 47; nom. pl. *aviddasû*, C. xii. 1, 3; besides we have *sabbavidû*, Dh. v. 353; *lokavidû*=lokavid of the Northern Buddhists, Lotus 860.

Bhavaṃ, 'Sir.'

	Singular.	Plural.
Nom.	*bhavaṃ.*	*bhavanto, bhonto, bhavantâ.*
Voc.	*bho, bhonta.*	*bhavanto, bhonto, bhante.*
Acc.	*bhavantaṃ, bhotaṃ.*	*bhavante, bhonte.*
Instr.	*bhavatâ, bhotâ, bhavantena.*	
D. G.	*bhavato, bhoto, bhavantassa.*	
Abl.	*bhavatâ, bhotâ.*	

The fem. shows the forms *bhavantî, bhavatî, bhotî*, Pl. *bhotiyo.*

(3). Stems in *in.*

Daṇḍin, 'a mendicant.'

	Singular.	Plural.
Nom.	*daṇḍî.*	*daṇḍino, daṇḍî.*
Voc.	*daṇḍi.*	*daṇḍino, daṇḍî.*
Acc.	*daṇḍinaṃ, daṇḍiṃ.*	*daṇḍino, daṇḍî.*
Instr.	*daṇḍinâ.*	*daṇḍîbhi, daṇḍîhi.*
D. G.	*daṇḍino, daṇḍissa.*	*daṇḍînaṃ.*
Abl.	*daṇḍinâ, daṇḍismâ, daṇḍimhâ.*	*daṇḍîbhi, daṇḍîhi.*
Loc.	*daṇḍini, daṇḍismiṃ, daṇḍimhi.*	*daṇḍîsu.*

At M. vi. 28, 11, we have an acc. pl. *brahmacariye*, of brahmacârin, 'holy;' and at Mahâparinibb. 16, we have the same passage with the v. l. *brahmacârayo*; the nom. pl. *sabrahmacârî* occurs Mahâparin. 5. *Dîpî*=dvîpin, 'a leopard,' forms the nom. pl. *dîpiyo*, Jât. xiv. 1, 27. The oblique cases of the plural have a short *i* only in verses: *pâṇinaṃ*, Dh. 135, *anuyoginaṃ*, Dh. v. 209. An instance of a nom. sing. with *ĭ* is *seṭṭhi*

=çreshṭin, 'a treasurer, merchant,' Jât. i. 120, 122, where all MSS. agree in the spelling.

Examples of an enlarged stem are *sâramatino* nom. sing.= sâramati, Mil. 420; *verinesu* from *verin*, 'hostile,' Dh. v. 197.

(4). Stems in *r*.

Satthâ=çâstṛi, 'the teacher.'

	Singular.	Plural.
Nom.	*satthâ.*	*satthâro.*
Voc.	*sattha, satthâ.*	*satthâro.*
Acc.	*satthâraṃ, sattharaṃ.*	*satthâro, satthâre.*
Instr.	*sattharâ, satthârâ, satthunâ.*	*satthârebhi, satthârehi.*
D. G.	*satthu, satthussa.*	*satthânaṃ, satthârânaṃ*
Abl.	*sattharâ, satthârâ.*	*satthârebhi, satthârehi.*
Loc.	*satthari.*	*satthâresu.*

Here also some stems have adopted the *a*-declension, as *sallakatta*=çalyakartṛi, 'a physician,' Mil. 110, Att. 208, to which Childers compares *nâhapita*=snâpitṛi, 'a barber;' *kattara* =kartṛi, 'a weak man,' in *kattaradaṇḍa*, M. v. 6, 2; *kattarasuppa*, M. vii. 1, 4; and *theta*=sthâtṛi, 'firm,' Gr. 5. In composition the base generally terminates in *u*, as *sotu*=çrotṛi, 'hearer,' Daṭh, vi. 6 (the gen. pl. *sotûnaṃ* occurs in a passage of the Mahâvagga of the Dîghanikâya, quoted I. O. C. 60); *bhattu*=bhartṛi, 'husband,' Jât. ii. 348; *mandhâtu*=mandhâtṛi, Jât. ii. 310. The voc. sing. *sattha* occurs Kacc. 116; the acc. *sattharaṃ*, Bv. xxii. 14; an instr. *satthâya*, Dh. 87; the gen. *satthussa*, Mah. 240.

Pitâ=pitṛi, 'a father.'

	Singular.	Plural.
Nom.	*pitâ.*	*pitaro.*
Voc.	*pita, pitâ.*	*pitaro.*
Acc.	*pitaraṃ, pituṃ.*	*pitaro, pitare.*
Instr.	*pitarâ, pitunâ, petyâ.*	*pitarebhi, pitarehi, pitûbhi, pitûhi.*
D. G.	*pitu, pituno, pitussa.*	*pitarânaṃ, pitânaṃ, pitûnaṃ, pitunnaṃ.*
Abl.	*pitarâ.*	*pitarebhi, pitarehi, pitûbhi, pitûhi.*
Loc.	*pitari.*	*pitaresu, pitûsu.*

Mâtâ=mâtṛi, 'a mother.'

	Singular.	Plural.
Nom.	*mâtâ.*	*mâtaro.*
Voc.	*mâta, mâtâ.*	*mâtaro.*
Acc.	*mâtaraṃ.*	*mâtaro, mâtare.*
Instr. Abl.	*mâtarâ, mâtuyâ, mâtyâ.*	*mâtarebhi, mâtarehi, mâtûbhi, mâtûhi.*
D. G.	*mâtu, mâtuyâ, mâtyâ.*	*mâtarânaṃ, mâtânaṃ, mâtûnaṃ, mâtunnaṃ.*
Loc.	*mâtari, mâtuyaṃ, mâtyaṃ, mâtuyâ, mâtyâ.*	*mâtaresu, mâtûsu.*

The acc. sing. *pituṃ* occurs Cariy. ii. 9, 3; the instr. *mâtyâ* and *petyâ*, Jât. 527, v. 3, 5; the gen. *mâtussa*, given by Kacc. 98, is not found anywhere else, and belongs most probably to a bâhuvrîhi (Torp. 33). An abl. *pitito* and *mâtito*, 'on father's and on mother's side,' occurs Kacc. 102, and in a passage from a commentary quoted by Alwis, Introd. xlv.

The nom. pl. *mâtârapitaro*, where both stems are inflected, occurs Ang. p. 121; the gen. *mâtâpitunnaṃ*, Ten Jât. 92. An acc. pl. *bhâte* occurs Dîp. 6, 21, 22.

The declension of *dhîtâ*, 'daughter,' is on the whole the same as that of *mâtâ*; we find, however, a voc. *dhîte*, Dh. 364, Jâṭ. iii. 21; and an acc. pl. *dhîtâ*, Jât. i. 240. In composition we have *dhîtiṭṭhâna*, Mah. 222; *dhîtuhetu*, Mil. 117.

Sakhi, 'a friend.'

	Singular.	Plural.
Nom.	*sakhâ.*	*sakhâyo, sakhâno, sakhino.*
Voc.	*sakha, sakhâ, sakhi, sakhî, sakhe.*	*sakhâyo, sakhâno, sakhino.*
Acc.	*sakhânaṃ, sakhaṃ, sakhâraṃ.*	*sakhî, sakhâyo, sakhâno, sakhino.*
Instr. Abl.	*sakhinâ.*	*sakhârebhi, sakhârehi, sakhebhi, sakhehi.*
D. G.	*sakhino, sakhissa.*	*sakhârânaṃ, sakhînaṃ.*
Loc.	*sakhe.*	*sakhâresu, sakhesu.*

The acc. *sakhaṃ* occurs Jât. ii. 348; an abl. *sakhârasmâ* is found Jât. iii. 534; *sakhito*, Att. 216. Acc. pl. *sakhî*, Att. 203.

(5). Stems in *s*.

Manas, 'the mind.'

Singular.

N. V. A.	*mano, manaṃ.*
Instr.	*manasâ, manena.*
D. G.	*manaso, manassa.*
Abl.	*manasâ, manasmâ, manamhâ.*
Loc.	*manasi, mane, manasmiṃ, manamhi.*

The plural of *manas* not in use. The others form it after the *a*-declension. The nom. acc. *manaṃ* occurs Dh. v. 96, Cariy. i. 8, 5; *rajaṃ*, 'dust,' Dh. v. 313, but *rajo* (with the adj. in the masc.), Dh. v. 125; *sumedhaṃ*, Dh. v. 208, but *sumedhaso*, Dh. v. 29; voc. *dummedha*, Dh. v. 394; a gen. *tapassa* occurs Jât. i. 293; nom. pl. *sumanâ*, Kh. 6.

Candramas, 'the moon,' becomes *candimâ*; jaras, 'old age,' *jarâ*; and apsaras, 'a celestial nymph,' *accharâ*; all these follow the *â*-declension.

The comparatives in *yo*, *iyyo*, follow the declension of *mano*; *seyyo*=çreyas, 'better;' *gariyo*=garîyas, from *guru*, 'heavy.'

Âyus, 'life.'

	Singular.	Plural.
N. V. A.	*âyu*, *âyuṃ*.	*âyûni*, *âyû*.
Instr.	*âyusâ*, *âyunâ*.	*âyûbhi*, *âyûhi*.
D. G.	*âyussa*, *âyuno*.	*âyûnaṃ*.
Loc.	*âyusi*, *âyuni*.	*âyûsu*.

The instr. *âyusâ* occurs Kh. 16; *âyunâ*, Dh. 288; the gen. *âyussa*, Mah. 220; *âyuno*, Dh. 128.

§ 15. Comparison of Adjectives.

Adjectives with vowel bases form their comparison in two ways:—

(1) By adding *tara* for the comparative and *tama* for the superlative.

(2) By adding *iyo*, *yo* for the comparative and *iṭṭha* for the superlative.

Thus, from *pâpa*, 'bad,' we can form *pâpatara*, *pâpatama* and *pâpiyo*, *pâpiṭṭha*, Kacc. 196. The comparative of no. 1 may be combined with the superlative of no. 2; thus we obtain *pâpiṭṭhatara*, C. i. 6, 2. Besides, the comparative of no. 2 may be increased by the addition of the suffix *ika*, which gives us *pâpiyyasika* in *tassapâpiyyasikâkamma*, M. ix. 6, 2; and with contraction *pâpissika*.

Adjectives terminating in *mant*, *vant* and *vin*, drop these suffixes before the comparative and superlative suffixes, as for inst. *guṇavâ* comp. *guṇiyo*, sup. *guṇiṭṭha*; *medhâvî* comp. *medhiyo*, sup. *medhiṭṭha*.

Some adjectives form their comp. and sup. from entirely different bases:

antika, 'near.'	Comp.	*nediyo*.	Sup.	*nediṭṭha*.
bâḷha, 'strong.'	„	*sâdhiyo*.	„	*sâdhiṭṭha*.
vuddha, 'old.'	„	*jeyyo*.	„	*jeṭṭha*.
appa, 'small.' } *yuvâ*, 'young.' }	„	*kaniyo*.	„	*kaniṭṭha*.
pasattha, 'excellent.'	„	*seyyo*.	„	*seṭṭha*.

§ 16. Pronominal Inflexion.

(1) *Personal Pronouns of the First and Second Persons.*

First Person.

	Singular.	Plural.
Nom.	*ahaṃ*.	*vayaṃ*, *mayaṃ*, *amhe*.
Acc.	*maṃ*, *mamaṃ*.	*asme*, *amhe*, *amhâkaṃ*.
Instr. Abl.	*mayâ*.	*amhebhi*, *amhehi*.
Dat. Gen.	*mama*, *mamaṃ*. *mayhaṃ*, *amhaṃ*.	*amhâkaṃ*, *amhaṃ*.
Loc.	*mayi*.	*amhesu*.

Second Person.

	Singular.	Plural.
Nom.	*tvaṃ, tuvaṃ.*	*tumhe.*
Acc.	*tvaṃ, tuvaṃ.*	*tumhe, tumhâkaṃ.*
	taṃ, tavaṃ.	
Instr. Abl.	*tvayâ, tayâ.*	*tumhebhi, tumhehi.*
Dat. Gen.	*tava, tavaṃ.*	*tumhâkaṃ, tumhaṃ.*
	tuyhaṃ, tumhaṃ.	
Loc.	*tvayi, tayi.*	*tumhesu.*

Besides, we have the enclitic forms: *me, te* for instr. dat. and gen. sing.; *no, vo* for acc. dat. and gen. pl.

The old form of the nom. pl. *vayaṃ* occurs Dh. 105, the acc. pl. *asme,* Jât. iii. 359. The acc. pl. *amhâkaṃ* and *tumhâkaṃ* are borrowed from the gen. The nom. pl. *amhe* and the gen. *amhaṃ* and *tumhaṃ, amhânaṃ* and *tumhânaṃ*, are only found in Kacc. 83, 84.

The enclitic forms *no* and *vo* may also be used for the nom., according to Kacc. 78.

(2) *The Demonstrative Pronoun.*

(a) Stem *ta,* 'this.'

Singular.

	Masc. and Neuter.		Feminine.
Nom.	*so, sa,*	*taṃ (tad).*	*sâ.*
Acc.	*taṃ,*	*taṃ (tad).*	*taṃ.*
Instr.	*tena.*		*tâya.*
Dat. Gen.	*tassa.*		*tassâ, tassâya, tissâ, tissâya, tâya.*
Abl.	*tasmâ,*	*tamhâ.*	*tâya.*
Loc.	*tasmiṃ,*	*tamhi.*	*tassaṃ, tâsaṃ, tissaṃ, tâyaṃ.*

Plural.

	Masc. and Neuter.	Feminine.
Nom. Acc.	*te, tâni.*	*tâ, tâyo.*
Instr. Abl.	*tebhi, tehi.*	*tâbhi, tâhi.*
Dat. Gen.	*tesaṃ, tesânaṃ.*	*tâsaṃ, tâsânaṃ.*
Loc.	*tesu.*	*tâsu.*

For all the forms beginning with *t* we may substitute the corresponding forms of the stem *na*. At Kacc. 89, the following forms are given: *nâya, naṃ, ne, nesu, namhi, nâhi.* Besides we have the stems *eta* and *ena*, which are inflected like *ta* and *na* respectively.

In the nom. sing. we generally have *so*, the form of the substantives, *sa* occurs Dh. v. 142, 267, 268. A gen. sing. masc. *taṣmassa* is found Anecd. 15, and at Mil. 136 all MSS. give *tâsaṃ* for the loc. sing. fem., which is no doubt a correct form, comp. *nesaṃ*, ib. 179.

(b) Stem *ima*, 'this.'

Singular.

	Masc. and Neuter.	Feminine.
Nom.	*ayaṃ, idam, imaṃ.*	*ayaṃ.*
Acc.	*imaṃ, idaṃ, imaṃ.*	*imaṃ.*
Instr.	*iminâ, anena.*	*imâya.*
D. G.	*imassa, assa.*	*imissâ, imissâya, imâya, assâ, assâya.*
Abl.	*imasmâ, imamhâ, asmâ.*	*imâya.*
Loc.	*imasmiṃ, imamhi, asmiṃ.*	*imissaṃ, imâsaṃ, imâyaṃ, assam.*

Plural.

	Masc. and Neuter.		Feminine.
N. A.	*ime,*	*imâni.*	*imâ, imâyo.*
In. Ab.	*imebhi, imehi, ebhi, ehi.*		*imâbhi, imâhi.*
D. G.	*imesaṃ, imesânaṃ, esaṃ, esânaṃ.*		*imâsaṃ, imâsânaṃ.*
Loc.	*imesu.*		*imâsu.*

In *tadaminâ* for *tadiminâ*, Vasala Sutta, v. 22, *i* is changed to *a* by dissimilation.

(c) Stem *amu*, 'that.'

Singular.

	Masc. and Neuter.		Feminine.
Nom.	*asu,*	*aduṃ.*	*asu.*
Acc.	*amuṃ,*	*aduṃ.*	*amuṃ.*
Instr.	*amunâ.*		*amuyâ.*
Dat. Gen.	*amussa.*		*amussâ, amuyâ.*
Abl.	*amusmâ, amumhâ.*		*amuyâ.*
Loc.	*amusmiṃ, amumhi.*		*amussaṃ, amuyaṃ.*

Plural.

	Masc. and Fem.	Neuter.
Nom. Acc.	*amû, amuyo.*	*amû, amûni.*
Instr. Abl.	*amûbhi, amûhi.*	
Dat. Gen.	*amûsaṃ, amûsânaṃ.*	
Loc.	*amûsu.*	

(3) *Relative Pronoun.*

Stem *ya*, 'which.'

Singular.

	Masc. and Neuter.	Feminine.
Nom.	*yo*, *yaṃ* (*yad*).	*yâ*.
Acc.	*yaṃ*, *yaṃ* (*yad*).	*yaṃ*.
Instr.	*yena*.	*yâya*.
Dat. Gen.	*yassa*.	*yassâ*, *yâya*.
Abl.	*yamhâ*.	*yâya*.
Loc.	*yasmiṃ*, *yamhi*.	*yassaṃ*, *yâyaṃ*.

Plural.

	Masc. and Neuter.	Feminine.
Nom.	*ye*, *yâni*.	*yâ*, *yâyo*.
Acc.	*ye*, *yâni*.	*yâ*, *yâyo*.
Instr.	*yebhi*, *yehi*.	*yâbhi*, *yâhi*.
Dat. Gen.	*yesaṃ*.	*yâsaṃ*.
Abl.	*yebhi*, *yehi*.	*yâbhi*, *yâhi*.
Loc.	*yesu*.	*yâsu*.

(4) *Interrogative Pronouns.*

Stem *ka*, 'which.'

The inflexion of this stem is like that of *ya* with the following exceptions: The nom. sing. neut. is *kiṃ*; in the dat. and gen. masc. and neut. sing. we have *kassa* and *kissa*, in the loc. *kasmiṃ*, *kamhi*, *kismiṃ* and *kimhi*.

The indefinite pronouns are formed by adding the particles *ci*, *api* and *cana* to the forms of the interrogative.

Besides, we have a number of words which although not being pronouns in the true sense of the word, still follow the pronominal inflexion: First of all, possessives like *madîya*, *mâmaka*, 'mine,' *amhadîya*, 'our,' would belong to this class, but of these we only find nominatives in our texts. Next come the adjectives composed with dṛiç, as *mâdisa*, 'like me;' *etâdisa* or *etârisa*, and *îdisa*, 'like this;' *kîdisa*, 'like what;' *cirassaṃ* for *cirassa*, 'long since,' seems to be a pronominal form.

By adding the suffixes *tara*, *tama* (already found in comparison of adjectives) to the interrogative stems, we obtain the pronominal adjectives *katara* and *katama*, which do not differ in their signification much from the single pronoun.

The other adjectives inflected according to the pronominal inflexion, are *sabba* and *vissa* = sarva and viçva, 'all;' *añña* = anya, 'other,' with its derivatives *aññatara*, *aññatama*; *itara*, 'other;' *uttara*, *uttama*, 'higher;' *adhara*, 'inferior;' *apara*, *para*, 'other;' *dakkhiṇa*, 'right;' *pubba*, 'former;' *amuka* and *asuka*, 'this.' The numeral for one, *eka*, also follow the same declension.

The grammarian Moggallâna (Alwis Catal., 184), asserts that these adjectives can also follow the regular declension of the *a*-stems, and gives some passages from unknown texts.

§ 17. Numerals.

(1) *Cardinals.*

1	*eka.*	5	*pañca.*
2	*dvi.*	6	*cha.*
3	*ti.*	7	*satta.*
4	*catu.*	8	*aṭṭha.*

9 *nava.*	19 *ekûnavîsaṃ, ekûnavîsati.*
10 *dasa.*	20 *vîsaṃ, vîsati.*
11 *ekâdasa, ekârasa.*	30 *tiṃsaṃ, tiṃsati.*
12 *dvâdasa, bârasa.*	40 *cattârîsaṃ, cattâlîsaṃ, tâlîsaṃ.*
13 *terasa.*	50 *paññâsaṃ, paññâsa.*
14 *catuddasa, coddasa, cuddasa.*	60 *saṭṭhi, saṭṭhiṃ.*
	70 *sattati, sattari.*
15 *pañcadasa.*	80 *asîti.*
16 *soḷasa.*	90 *navuti.*
17 *sattadasa, sattarasa.*	100 *sataṃ.*
18 *aṭṭhâdasa, aṭṭhârasa.*	1000 *sahassaṃ.*

The forms *vîsaṃ*, *tiṃsaṃ*, etc., show that the termination *ti* of the Saṃskṛit, can be replaced in Pâli by the anusvâra. We find the anusvâra occasionally also where it has no right to be, as in *dvâdasaṃ*, Mah. 8; *saṭṭhiṃ* = shashṭi, Dh. 211. When the nasal is dropped the remaining *a* may be lengthened.

The intermediate numerals between *vîsaṃ* and *tiṃsaṃ*, etc., are regular, with the only exception that instead of *dvi* we generally find *dvâ*, *bâ* (or *dva*, *ba* before a double consonant), as in *dvâvîsati*, *bâvîsati*, *dvattiṃsa*, *battiṃsa*, *dvenavuti*, and instead of *ti*, *te* as in *tevîsati*. For caturaçîti we have *cullâsîti*, for pañcaviṃçati *paṇṇuvîsaṃ*, Jât. iii. 138.

From *cha* we have a plural *chaḷâni*, Dîp. 108, and for twelve *dviccha* = dvishash, Ab. 195.

About the declension of *eka*, see the Pronouns.

Dvi and the synonymous *ubho* have the following inflexion:

N. A.	*dve, duve.*	*ubho, ubhe.*
I. A.	*dvîbhi, dvîhi.*	*ubhobhi, ubhohi, ubhebhi, ubhehi.*
D. G.	*dvinnaṃ, duvinnaṃ.*	*ubhinnaṃ.*
Loc.	*dvîsu.*	*ubhosu, ubhesu.*

Ubho = Skt. ubhau is one of the few rests of the Dual remaining in Pâli (see above, p. 65).

In the numerals *ti* and *catu* we have separate forms for the fem., very much in the same way as in Skt.:

Masc. and Neuter.

Nom. Acc.	*tayo,*	*tîni.*	*cattâro, caturo,*	*cattâri.*
Instr. Abl.	*tîbhi,*	*tîhi.*	*catubbhi, catûbhi, catûhi.*	
Dat. Gen.	*tiṇṇaṃ, tiṇṇannaṃ.*		*catuṇṇaṃ.*	
Loc.	*tîsu.*		*catûsu.*	

Feminine.

Nom. Acc.	*tisso.*	*catasso.*
Instr. Abl.	*tîbhi, tîhi.*	*catubbhi, catûbhi, catûhi.*
Dat. Gen.	*tissannaṃ.*	*catassannaṃ.*
Loc.	*tîsu.*	*catûsu.*

Pañca forms the instr. abl. *pañcahi,* Gen. Dat. *pañcannaṃ,* Loc. *pañcasu,* and this is the declension all numerals in *a* follow.

The numerals in *i* are declined like the fem. *i*-stems, *sataṃ* and *sahassaṃ* like neuters in *aṃ*.

Sataṃ and *sahassaṃ,* in conjunction with a noun, can be joined to nouns in the following ways:

(1) With a noun in the gen. pl., as *itthînaṃ pañca satâni,* 'five hundred women.'

(2) With a noun in the nom. pl. (*sataṃ* being either in the sing. or in the pl.), as *pañcasataṃ yatî,* '500 yatis,' or *pañcasatâ bhikkhû,* '500 mendicants.'

(3) With a noun in the sing., as *chacattâlîsaṃ vassaṃ atikamma,* 'after the lapse of 146 years.'

(4) As a compound, the numeral being the last part, as *gâthâsataṃ*, '100 stanzas.'

(5) As a compound, the numeral being the first part, as *sahassajaṭilâ*, 'a thousand jaṭilas.'

Another form of *sahassa* is *sahassî*, which is used promiscuously as a masc. and fem. in connection with *cakkavâla* or *vasudhâ*, &c., as *dasasahassî-cakkavâle*, 'in ten thousand worlds,' Dh. 94. Sometimes the subst. is omitted, and *dasasahassî* is treated like a fem. noun, as *dasasahassî pakampati*, 'ten thousand worlds quake,' comp. Senart, Mahâvastu 373.

The Ordinals.

The Ordinals for five, and from seven upwards, are formed by adding the suffix *ma* to the cardinal, as *pañcama*, 'the fifth,' *sattama*, 'the seventh;' the fem. terminates in *î*, the neuter in *aṃ*, and they are declined like the corresponding substantives.

The Ordinal forms of the first numerals are: one, *paṭhama*; two, *dutiya*; three, *tatiya*; four, *catuttha*; six, *chaṭṭha*; *saṭṭha* (only known from Kacc. 200) and *chaṭṭhama*, Jât. i. 22, Bv. ii. 142.

From twenty upwards we have two forms, one by adding *ma* to the cardinal in *ti*, as *vîsatima*, 'the twentieth;' and one by dropping the termination *ti*, as *vîsa*, *tiṃsa*, &c.

From *sataṃ*, *sahassaṃ*, we have the ordinals *satama*, *sahassama*.

Besides, we have fem. ordinals in *î* to designate the day of the month; as *pañcamî*, 'the fifth day;' *ekâdasî*, 'the eleventh day,' &c.

§ 18. Conjugation.

The division of the Pâli Verb, as established by the native grammarians, is on the whole the same as that of the Skt. They admit of seven classes, of which the first again is divided into four conjugations; these correspond to the classes i., vi., ii., iii. of the Saṃskṛit grammarians, and the other six classes to the remaining Saṃskṛit classes in the following order, vii., iv., v., ix., viii., x. . Thus we obtain the following divisions of the Pâli Verb:—

First class:—(a) Verbs terminating in ĭ, ŭ or a consonant, which take guṇa and the vowel *a*: √ *bhû*, *bhavâmi*, 'to be.'

(b) Verbs ending in consonants which take the vowel *a*, but no guṇa: √ *tud*, *tudâmi*, 'to pierce.'

(c) Verbs ending in vowels which take guṇa, but add the personal endings without an intervening vowel: √ *i*, *emi* 'to go.'

(d) Verbs forming their bases by reduplication: √ *hû* *juhomi*, 'to sacrifice.'

The third division (c) is given in the Dhâtumañjûsâ as *huvâdayo*, where *hû* is another form of the root *bhû*, 'to be,' forming its present *homi*.

Second class:—Verbs taking the *a*-vowel and inserting a nasal before the final consonant of the root: √ *rudh*, *rundhâmi*, 'to restrain.'

Third class:—Verbs adding the suffix *ya*, *yâ* to the root: √ *div*, *dibbâmi*, 'to play.'

Fourth class:—Verbs adding the suffixes *ṇâ*, *ṇu* (which becomes *ṇo* by guṇa) or *uṇâ* to the root: √ *çru*, *suṇâmi* or *suṇomi*, 'to hear;' √ *âp*, *pâpuṇâmi*, 'to attain.'

Fifth class:—Verbs ending in a vowel, which add the suffix *nâ* to the root: √ *krî*, *kiṇâmi*, 'to buy.'

Sixth class:—Verbs ending in a consonant, which add *u* (or *o* by guṇa) to the root: √ *tan*, *tanomi*, 'to stretch.'

Seventh class:—Verbs adding the suffix *aya* (or *e* by contraction) to the root: √ *cur*, *corayâmi* or *coremi*, 'to steal.'

Verbs have two voices, the *Parassapada* or Transitive, and the *Attanopada* or Intransitive; the use of the latter is much more restricted than in Saṃskṛit, most of the Attanopada verbs having adopted the Parassapada terminations.

We distinguish in Pâli, as in Saṃskṛit, special and general tenses. It must, however, be observed that the special and general bases very often take the place of one another, as will be shown hereafter.

Special tenses:—

(1) Present Indicative, Subjunctive, Optative and Imperative.
(2) Imperfect.

General tenses:—

(1) Perfect.
(2) Aorist.
(3) Future.
(4) Conditional.

Terminations of the Present Indicative.

Parassapada.		Attanopada.	
Sing.	Pl.	Sing.	Pl.
mi	*ma*	*e*	*mhe* (*mahe*, *mha*)
si	*tha*	*se*	*vhe*
ti	*nti*	*te*	*nte*, *re*

These terminations are very similar to the corresponding ones in Saṃskṛit. In the first pers. pl. of the Attan. we sometimes find the fuller form in *mahe*, as *bhasmîbhavâmahe*, Mah. 6; the termination *mha* shortened from *mhe* occurs in *dadamha*, Dh. 188, *maññamha*, Dh. 205 (the long *â* is crasis for the *i* of the following *iti*, see above, p. 60). Instead of *ante* in the third pers. pl. we frequently meet with the termination *are*, especially in old texts, metrical as well as prosaïcal, as *miyyare* = mriyante, 'they die,' Das. Jât. 34; *udiccare* from udîksh, 'they looked,' M. I. 15, 6; *abhikîrare*, 'they overwhelm,' Jât. iii. 57. This *are* is most probably the vedic termination *re* of the third pers. pl. âtmanep. as in çriṇvire; it also exists in Prâk. Hem. iii. 142.

We have to consider first the verbs that add the terminations immediately to the root (which form the second class in Saṃskṛit, in Pâli division (c) of the first class). The paradigm adopted by the native grammarians is *hû* = bhû, 'to be.' It forms its present as follows:—

homi	*homa*
hosi	*hotha*
hoti	*honti*

Other roots belonging to this class are those terminating in *â*, like *yâ*, 'to go,' *vâ*, 'to blow,' which have entirely the same inflexion as in Skt., only that they shorten the *â* in the third pers. pl., *yanti*=Skt. yânti. Besides, the root *yâ* may follow the third class, as in *yâyanti*, M. v. 9, 4. *Ṭhâ*=sthâ, 'to stand,' forms its present *ṭhâti* and *tiṭṭhati*, e.g., *ṭhâta*, Dh. 123, *saṃṭhâti*, Dh. 429; from *dâ* we have a present, *dâti*, Kacc. 264, imper. first pers. pl. *nipadâmase*, Jât. iii. 120 (explained by the commentary *nikârapakârâ upasaggâ dâmase ti attho*). *Pajjhâti*, Jât. iii. 534, is most probably derived from *jhâ* = kshâ, 'to decay,' comp. *pajjhâyi*, *pajjhâyasi*, Suttavibh. i. 19, ii. 5.

From *dhyâ* we have *pajjhâyanto*, 'groaning,' Mil. 5, if Trenckner's translation is correct, and according to Senart, Mahâvastu 377, also the present *âvajjati* and *âvajjeti*, 'to consider,' which would have dropped the aspiration. From *snâ*, 'to bathe,' we have an imper. *nahâhi* belonging to this class, Jât. ii. 325. From *ṭhâti* and *dhâti* = *dadhâti* we come to the forms *ṭhahati* and *dahati* which are in very frequent use in Pâli.

Of verbs terminating in *i* we have to mention here besides *i* and *çî*, which belong to this class also in Skt., nî, 'to lead,' çri, 'to lean,' ji, 'to conquer,' ḍî and ḷî, 'to fly.' *I* seems to form its present very much as in Skt., for the first and second pers. pl. of course we get *ema*, *etha*, instead of imas, ita; for the third pl. Childers adduces a form *samudayanti* from Brahmajâlas. Atth. which is formed from *samudenti* by false analogy. In the present *vyapanenti* quoted by Minayeff, p. xxxii. from Udânagâthâ and in *vassûpanâyika*, M. iii. 2, 2, we have derivations from *i* with the prepositions *apan* and *upan* respectively, which make them look as though they were derived from *nî*, comp. Vinaya Texts, i. xxxvii. A present *ayati* belonging to the *bhû*-class is given in Dhm., but has not yet been found in any text.

Çî forms its present *semi*, Cariy. ii. 2, 3, third pl. *senti*, Dh. 28; in the part. we have *semâna*, Jât. i. 180, Mah. 49; *sayamâna*, Att. 218.

Nî forms *neti* and *nayati* according to Kacc. 261; part. *upanento*, Dh. 154; gerund *apanetvâ* instead of °*nîtvâ* by false analogy.

Çri forms a present *apasseti*, C. vi. 20, 2, comp. *apassena* for apaçrayana.

Ji has the present *jayati*, *jeti* and *jinâti*, Kaçc. 261; opt. *jeyya* for *jayeyya*, Dh. v. 103.

Ḍî (and ḷî) forms its present *ḍeti*, Gr. 136. There are two compounds of this root, *oḍḍeti* and *uḍḍeti*, the explanation of which causes considerable difficulty. *Oḍḍeti* occurs in the signification, 'to place, to lay nets,' Jât. i. 274, ii. 443, 5, 52, 153, 183, 238, Suttavibh. i. 22 (v. l. *oṭṭi*, Buddh. *oḍḍhî ti abhimukhaṃ ṭhapesi*), *uḍḍeti*, 'to cast a net,' Ang. i. 24, 4. Morris, in a note to this last passage, identifies the two forms, and he is no doubt right, but I believe *uḍḍeti* to be the original one, and *oḍḍeti* a later change. Instead of *omâna*, Jât. ii. 443, vs. 1, we ought to read *ḍemâna*. A causative of the same root is *uṭṭepeti*, 'to frighten away,' M. i. 51, comp. uḍḍâpita, Çatr. 10, 91, and perhaps *niḍḍâyati*, Jât. i. 215, *niddâpeti*, C. vii. 1, 2; but these two might also belong to dâ, dyati. In Prâk. we have uḍḍibiyaṃ, Pâiyal. 182.

The root brû, which is generally given as paradigm of this class in Skt., shows the following conjugation in Pâli:—

Parassapada.		Attanopada.	
brûmi	*brûma*	*brave*	*brûmhe*
brûsi	*brûtha*	*brûse*	*brûvhe*
brûti, bravîti	*bravanti*	*brûte*	*bravante*

The root han has *hanti* in the third pers. sing., but *hanati*, Mil. 220, *hananti* in the third pl., Dh. 64, for Skt. ghnanti.

Vac forms *vatti* and *vacati*, according to Saddanîti, but these forms have not yet been found in any text.

The root as, 'to be,' has the following inflexion:—

asmi, amhi	*asma, amha*
asi	*attha*
atthi	*santi*

At Jât. iii. 309 we have a curious first pers. pl., *amhase*, which looks like an imperf. attanop. but is used like a present.

The synonymous root *acchati* is now proved beyond doubt to belong to âs, from which it proceeds through the aorist *acchi*, see Trenckner, Pâli Misc. 61, Pischel, Gött. Anz. 1865, p. 627, Torp 88. We find the compound *samacchati*, in the original signification, 'to sit down,' Jât. ii. 67. The aorist *acchi* occurs Dh. 158, Suttavibh. i. 35.

The present *pâheti*, 'to send,' also belongs to this class, although it is given by the grammarians among the *svâdayo* and *tanâdayo*. The *â* in the first syllable shows that it is only deduced by false analogy from the aorist *pâhesi*= Skt. prâhaishît, but it is considered as a genuine present in Pâli.

As a paradigm of division (d) of the first class, I give here the conjugation of the root *hu*, 'to sacrifice.'

juhomi.	*juhoma.*
juhosi.	*juhotha.*
juhoti, juvhati.	*juhonti, juvhanti.*

Besides, there seems to be a new root, *juh* taken from the special base, and inflected with the vowel *a*, as in *juhamâna*, Jât. ii. 399; and from this is also derived the subst. *juhana*, 'sacrifice,' Jât. i. 493, wrongly spelt *jûhana*, Gr. 16.

Other roots belonging to this class are those ending in *â*, some of which I have already mentioned; *hâ* forms the present *jahâti*, but we find also *vijahati*, Dh. 99, 261, from a new root, *jah*.

Dâ and dhâ can also have the regular forms *dadâti* and *dadhâti*, besides the new ones mentioned above, and from *dadâmi* is also derived the contracted form *dammi* = dadmi, pl. *damma*, Dh. 123, 129; Jât. i. 127, etc. Besides we have a present *demi*, which shows exactly the same inflexion as *emi*, 'I go;' Childers derives it either from the Skt. dayate, or by false analogy from the imper. *dehi detu*, but I confess that none of these explanations seems to me quite satisfactory.

From dhâ we have *nidheti*, Kh. 12 ; *nidhetuṃ*, Khuddasikkhâ, xxxi. 2 ; and besides a distracted form *daheti* (analogous to *dahati* from *dhâti*) in the aorist *pidahesi*, Mah. 4, and the future *paridahessati*, Dh. v. 9. Pass. *antaradhâyati*.

From sthâ we have the imp. *uṭṭhehi*, Rev. v. 3 ; Dîp. 60 ; *niṭṭhâyati*, C. v. 26, generally *niṭṭhâti*. From hnu, Kacc. 135 gives the present *hanute*, but the Dhm. omits this root altogether.

The division (*a*) of the first class has considerably encroached on most of the other classes. Nearly all the roots terminating in *u* or a consonant, and belonging to the second class of the Skt. have migrated into this class in Pâli: lih forms *lehati*, Jât. i. 19 ; *lehentâ*, Jât. ii. 31 ; Suttavibh, i. 46 ; duh : *dohati*, Kacc. 144 ; but *duhanti*, ib. 141 ; rud : *rodati* and *rudati*, Jât. iii. 214 ; *rodâmi*, Das. Jât. 33. Vetti, from vid, 'to know,' is entirely lost in Pâli, and generally replaced by *jânâti*. We find, however, a present *vindati* formed according to the 6th class of the Skt., and *vijjati* = vidyate ; besides *vedeti* and *vediyati*, Mil. 60 ; Suttavibh. ii. 167 ; Part. *vedayita*, Mil. 60. From jâgar, 'to watch,' we have the present *jâgarati*, Dh. 8, 11, 41, and *jaggati*, Dh. 201 ; Jât. iii. 403 ; comp. the Prâk. forms jâgaraï and jaggaï, Hem. iv. 80 ; from daridrâ, 'to be poor,' the Dhm. gives *daliddati ;* but this form has not yet been found in any text. In some cases the *e* is only due to false analogy, as in the fut. *gahessati*, and aorist *aggahesi*, from gṛih, see Childer's 'Corrigenda,' s. v.

Ḍaç, 'to bide,' forms *ḍasanto*, *ḍasitvâ* and *ḍaṃsento*, *ḍaṃsetvâ*, *ḍasâpetvâ*, *ḍaṃsâpetvâ*, Ten. Jât. 42, 43, 44, 54.

Dhmâ, 'to blow,' forms *dhamati* and *dhameti ;* besides we

have a reduplicated form *dhamâdhamayati*, Mil. 117; *niddhamana*, 'a water-course,' is also derived from this root.

The root *vî* or *ve*, 'to weave,' is given in the Dhm. among those that follow the first conjugation, and indeed we find an infinitive *vetuṃ*, C. vi. 2, 6; a present *abbeti* occurs, Jât. iii. 34, where Fausböll has altered it into *appeti*, comp. Trenckner, P. M. 64. A new present *vinâti*, formed according to the fifth class, occurs Jât. ii. 302; and besides we have the regular passive *vîyati* or *viyyati*, Pât. 11.

Vad, 'to speak,' supplying the lost special tenses of vac forms its present *vadati* and *vadeti*. The Dhm. only gives a root vad with the signification 'to praise' following *corayâmi*. Besides, *vajj* may be substituted throughout all the tenses, according to Kacc. 254 (derived, no doubt, from the opt. *vajju*, Jât. ii. 322), e.g. *vajjâsi*, Jât. iii. 443, comp. vivâdyanti, Mahâvastu, p. 378.

Tas = tras, 'to tremble,' forms its present regularly *tasati*, Dh. 24; we find, however, an aorist *vitthâsi*, Kamm. 4, a present *vitthâyati*, M. i. 76, 3; C. x. 17, 3, and a participle *vitthata* Mil. 36; for *vitthata* comp. Prâk. hittha, Hem. ii. 136, P. Goldschmidt's remarks 'Setubandha,' ii. 42; *vitthâsi* reminds one of a form trâhi, Lalitavistara, p. 286, which I have corrected into trâsi (Der Dialekt der Gâthâs des Lal. p. 284), and *vitthâyanti* seems to be formed after the false analogy of this aorist in the same way as *pâheti* from *pâhesi*.

Tud forms *vitûdati* with lengthening *nittûdana*, Mahâparin. 54, besides *vitudaṃ* (?) Dh. 146; from *khan*, 'to dig,' we have an irregular inf. *nikhâtuṃ*, Cariy. iii. 6, 16.

Ruh forms *abhirohati*, *abhirûhati* with lengthening, and even *abhiruhati*.

Bhî, 'to fear,' forms *bhâyati*, comp. Hem. iv. 53. The reduplicated form bibheti is entirely lost in Pâli. The Imper. *bhâtha*, Jât. i. 26, is contracted from *bhâyatha*.

Svap, 'to sleep,' forms *supati*; Part. *sumanta*, Mil. 368.

Vyath, 'to tremble,' is also given under this class in Dhm., but I have only found it under the form *vedhati*. At C. vii. 4, 6, Oldenberg has suggested to read *vyathati* for the senseless *vyâdhati*. The causative is *vedheti*, Trenckner, P. M. 76.

The second class of the Pâli, corresponding originally to the seventh of the Skt., forms its present after the fashion of those verbs of the sixth class which adopt *n*: so we obtain from *rudh* a present *rundhâmi*, just as we have from *vid*, *vindâmi*. Kacc. 238 gives besides the forms *rundhiti*, *rundhîti*, *rundheti*, of which the last occurs also in the imper. *rundhehi*, Cariy. iii. 10, 7 (where, however, the corresponding passage of the Jât. i. 332, reads *randhehi*). About the passive *rumh*, see above, p. 39.

The other roots belonging to this class, as muc, 'to release,' chid, 'to cut,' lip, 'to smear,' bhuj, 'to eat,' are regular.

The third class comprises the verbs that take the suffix *ya* (with assimilation of *y* to the consonant terminating the root). Some of the verbs belonging to this class are real passives, as *vijjati*, 'to be found, to exist,' pass. of *vidati*; *udriyati*, 'to gò to ruin,' from dar, dṛiṇâti, M. iii. 8, 1; Suttavibh. ii. 254. Others have adopted the meaning of actives, as *bujjhati* from budh, 'to know, to understand,' *sibbati* from *sîv*, 'to sew,' *dajjati* is most probably not the Skt. dadyate only given by grammarians, but a derivation from the opt. *dajjâ*, just as *vajjati* from *vajjâ* (see above, p. 102).

Mar forms the present *marati* and *mîyati* or *miyyati*. At Saddhammop. vs. 139, we find *marîyati*, which certainly is not classical.

Jar, 'to decay,' forms *jîyati* or *jiyyati* and *jîrati;* besides we have *jûrasi* in a passage quoted by Childers, J. R. A. S. xi. 110, from an unknown author. Comp. Prâk. jûraï, Hem. iv. 132.

Çar, 'to throw down,' forms *seyyasi* = çîryasi, Jât. i. 174. Part. *visiṇṇa* = viçîrṇa.

Lû, 'to reap,' forms *lâyati*, Das. 31, Jât. i. 215; *lâyeti*, Suttavibh. i. 64; *lâveti*, with change of *y* to *v*, Kacc. 262; *lâpayati*, Mah. 61, and the regular *lunâti*, Kacc. 238.

Gâ, 'to sing,' forms *gâyati*, Dh. 85; imper. *gâhi*, Jât. iii. 507.

The fourth class corresponds to the fifth of the Skt.; but most of the verbs belonging to it can also form their present according to the ninth, by adding the suffix nâ to the root. From çru, 'to hear,' we have the present *suṇoti* and *suṇâti*, imper. *suṇohi* and *suṇâhi*, inf. *suṇituṃ*, Mil. 91. From ci, 'to collect,' we have *cinâti*, Dh. 209; *vinicchinati*, Dh. 377; *ocinâyatu*, Cariy. iii. 6, 7; *saṃcinoti*, Att. 200; part. *saṃcayanto*, according to the first class, Mah. 127. Roots ending in a consonant can assimilate the *n* to this consonant, or insert *u* before the Suff. *nu* or *nâ*, e.g. *pappoti*, *pâpuṇoti* and *pâpuṇâti*, from √âp, 'to attain,' *sakkoti* and *sakkunâti* (where the second *k* is due to the false analogy of *sakkoti*), from √çak, 'to be able;' *sakkâti* occurs Saddhammop. v. 385, and a shortened form *sakkati* is induced by Childers from Nâvâ S. and Saddanîti.

Gar, 'to sound,' forms *anugiṇâti* = anugṛiṇâti, 'he answers,' Kacc. 139. Besides we have *uggirati*, 'to rattle,' Jât. i. 150; Pât. 18.

Abhisambhuṇoti, 'to obtain,' Lotus, 313, Pât. vii., is referred by Childers to the root bhṛî of the Dhâtupâṭha, and this explanation is adopted with some hesitation by Senart Mahâvastu 406. The Dhm. gives an especial root *sambhu*.

Sumbhoti, Kacc. 238, is perhaps identical with Skt. çubh, çubhnâti, 'to kill,' comp. Mahâvastu, 381. The Dhm. gives a root *sumbh*, 'to beat,' following the first class, and Jât. iii. 185, we have *sumhâmi*, v. l. *sumbhâmi* explained by *paharâmi*.

From var, 'to cover,' we have several forms according to this class; Trenckner, P. M. 63, gives the following: *vaṇimhase*, Jât. ii. 137; *apâpuṇanti*, It. 84, v. 2; *vaṇomi*, Jât. 513, v. 14; *âvunitvâ*, 'having pierced,' Cariy. iii. 12, 2; *saṃvuṇoti* and *saṃvuṇâti*, Kacc. 238. But it can also follow the first class as *vivarati* (*vivuṇâti* seems not to exist), *saṃvarati*, Mil. 152; *pâpurati* and *pârupati*, 'to dress;' *avapurati*, F. J. 29; *avâpuriyati*, Jât. i. 63 (comp. *avâpurana*, 'a key,' Ab. 222).

The fifth class corresponds to the ninth of the Skt., but includes also some verbs belonging originally to other classes. The Pâli grammarians reckon among this class several verbs which originally belong to the fifth class of the Skt., like *cinâti*, 'to collect,' *dhunâti*, 'to shake,' Skt. cinoti, dhunoti. About *jinâti* see above, p. 98. From *pû*, 'to purify,' we have *opunâti*, Dh. v. 252; Jât. i. 467; Mahâparin. 49. From *kiṇâti*, 'to buy,' we have an irregular inf. *ketuṃ*, Jât. iii. 282.

Mush, 'to steal,' forms its present *musati*, Ras. 32; *pamussati* derives most probably not from *mush* but from *smṛish*, see above, p. 58.

Aç, 'to eat,' forms *asnâti*, Mettânisaṃsâ, vs. 8; imper. *asnâtha*, Mahâparin. 59.

Mâ, 'to measure,' forms *minâti*, caus. *minâpeti*, Jât. ii. 378; *nimimhase*, Jât. ii. 369, Dh. 417.

Badh forms *bandhati* instead of *badhnâti* with a metathesis similar to that of *rundhati* = runaddhi; *lag*, 'to stick,' forms *laggati* = lagnâti, besides *lagati* after the first. From *ma h*, 'to grind,' we have *abhimatthati* = abhimathnâti.

Jñâ forms *jânâti* regularly; from *gṛih* we have *gaṇhâti* and *gaṇhati*, Dh. 160.

Other verbs following this class are *mun* = man, 'to think,' in *munâti*, comp. Hem. iv. 7; Fausb. S. N. 169; and *thun* = stan, 'to thunder' in *thunanti* (meaning 'to proclaim,' which points really to a confusion of the roots stan and stu, as one would think from Dhm.), Rev. 3; *anutthunâti*, Dh. 28, 323. From the same root we have *thanayaṃ*, Mahâsamayas. vs. 23; *thanita*, Att. 210; Jât. i. 64; *nitthananta*, Jât. ii. 362; *nitthanamâna*, Jât. i. 463.

The sixth class corresponds to the eighth of the Skt. In Pâli, however, in this case the root *kar*, 'to do,' can form its present quite regularly in the following way:

karomi.	*karoma.*
karosi.	*karotha.*
karoti.	*karonti.*

Besides, we have a form *kummi* for the first pers. sing., Jât. ii. 435, to which we may compare kurumi, Lalitavistara, 270. In the attanopada we have *kurute*, Dh. 9, 39, Mah. 219; and, besides, *kubbate*, *kubbati*, Kacc. 261; *vikubbati*, Jât. iii. 114; *tan* has *tanomi* regularly.

The Dhm. reckons several more roots to this class, of which some have been dealt with before, and others do not occur in any text, so that we need not mention them here.

The seventh class comprises the denominative verbs, the causatives, and a few primitive verbs, which have migrated into it from other classes. The inflexion of these is the same as of the verbs terminating in *i* or *î* which belong to the first class, as ji, çî, nî, etc.; *aya* can always be contracted into *e*, and also *ayi* of the past and future undergoes very often the same change. Even verbs in *âyati* can be contracted, as *paleti* for *palâyati*, Dh. v. 49.

Among this class I also reckon verbs like *âgilâyati*, 'to be weary, to pain,' C. vii. 4, 2, which is given by the Dhm. as belonging to the third. A doubtful word is *saṃkâyati*, C. x. 18, with the v. l. *sahâyati*.

Primitive verbs that occasionally take the suffix of this class are vac in *vacehi*, Dh. 159, vad in *vademi*, *vadehi*, Ras. 21, *dajj* in *dajjehi*, M. vi. 23, 3; Suttavibh. i. 217, tud in *vitudeti*, Suttavibh i. 105. About *vediyati* and *vedayita* see above, p. 101.

Imperative.

Parassapada.		Attanopada.	
mi	*ma*	*e*	*mase*
hi or °	*tha*	*ssu*	*vho*
tu	*nti*	*taṃ*	*ntaṃ*

Mi is most probably transferred from the present by false analogy. In the second person the short form without suffix is not so frequent as in Skt. We find *hi* also in such cases where we are not accustomed to see it in Skt., as in *gaṇhâhi* for *gaṇha*=gṛibṇa. From gacch we have *gacchahi*, Kacc. 248, besides *gacchâhi*. *Paṭimâse*, Dh. v. 379, is contracted from *paṭimâsaya*. The termination *tha* of the second pers. pl. is evidently taken from the present, e.g., *etha*, *passatha*, Dh. v. 171, *brûtha*, Jât. iii. 520. From aç, 'to eat,' we have *asnâtha* Mahâparin. 59.

The termination *ssu* of the second pers. sing. attanop., derived from Skt. sva, is very frequent even in verbs which follow the parassapada inflexion, e.g., *bhavassu*, Dh. v. 371, *pilandhassu*, Mil. 337, *âsassu*, 'relate,' Gr. 118 for *âsasassu*, comp. Kacc. 288; third pers. *labhataṃ*, Mahâpar. 62. The termination *mase* of the first pers. pl. is either very old or very modern (comp. for the first eventuality Kuhn, p. 101, for the second, Torp, p. 47); besides we have one instance of a form terminating in *mahaṃ*, *gacchâmahaṃ*, Dh. 86. For the curious form in *vho* of the second pers. pl. (we would expect *vhaṃ*= Skt. dhvaṃ) I can only adduce one example, *nivattavho*, Jât. ii. 358.

The form of the root is the same in the imperative as in the indicative. Thus we have from çru, second pers. sing., *suṇohi*, Att. 134; from kar, second pers. sing., *karohi*, Dh. 42; besides *kuru*, Mah. 18, 61, second pl. *karotha*, first pers. pl. attan. *karomase*, Jât. ii. 258. From dâ we have the Skt. form *dehi*, besides *dadâhi*, Jât iii. 109; *dajja* and even *dajjehi*, M. vi. 23, 3.

From *as* a second pers. sing. *âhi* is given by Childers and Minayeff, but has not yet been found in any text. The form is always expressed by *bhava*, *bhavassu*, or *hohi*, Dh. 187.

About the existence of the attanop. forms of kar and dâ given by Minayeff, § 178, 179, I feel very doubtful.

Subjunctive.

The subjunctive in Pâli has been discovered by Pischel, K.Z. xxiii. 424, who adduces a few examples from Dh. and Jât. It differs from the indicative only by the lengthening of the vowel *a*. Farther instances are *paṭibhaṇâti*, Jât. iii. 404, *hanâsi*, Jât. iii. 199, and perhaps *dahâsi*, *dahâti*, Fausb. S. N. 161, 169.

Optative.

Parassapada.		Attanopada.	
eyyâmi, e, eyya	*eyyâma, ema*	*eyyaṃ*	*eyyâmhe*
eyyâsi, e, eyya	*eyyâtha, etha*	*etho*	*eyyavho*
eyya, e	*eyyuṃ*	*etha*	*eraṃ*

This form of the optative originated from contraction of the optative suffix *îya* with the *a* of the first class, but it is in use with the other classes as well. When stems end in a vowel, this vowel is dropped before the *e* of the termination, as, e.g., *dadeyya*, and even *deyya*, from *dadâti*.

Roots terminating in *â*, and following division (c) of the first class form their optative by inserting *y*, as *yâyeyya*, from yâ, Pât. 110, *nhâyeyya* from *nahâ*=snâ, *nibbâyeyya* from nirvâ, 'to be extinguished;' from the last we have besides an abbreviated form *parinibbaye*, Das. 6.

The forms of the sing. in *e* are frequent enough in older texts, as *ânaye* (first pers.), Jât. i. 308; *labhe*, Cariyâp. i. 1, 9; *rode*, Jât. iii. 165; *nivase* (first and second pers.), Jât. iii. 259, 262; *pâpune* (third pers.), C. vii. 4, 8; *dade*, Cariy. i. 3, 8. In Khuddasikkhâ we find even a third sing. *de*.

The termination *eyya* of the first pers. originated from *eyyaṃ* after the nasal had been dropped; it is a form of the parassap. identical with the Skt. eyam, as we can see from instances like *deseyyaṃ*, Dhp. 119, *puccheyyaṃ*, Pât. 1, etc.

The first sing. in *eyyâmi*, as far as I know, is only given by grammarians as *heyyâmi*, *bhaveyyâmi*, *huveyyâmi*, from Rûpasiddhi, at Alwis Introd. 48, in the second we have *e* and *eyyâsi*, as *sikkheyyâsi*, Jât. i. 162, *âhareyyâsi*, Dh. 248, once *eyya* in *yâjeyya*, Jât. iii. 515; in the third *e* and *eyya*. One instance of the fuller form *eyyâti* occurs: *jâneyyâti*, C. vii. 3, 4. In the first pers. pl. we have *emasi*, *emu*, and *ema*, as *vidhamemasi*, Jât. iii. 261, *passemu*, Jât. iii. 495, *jânemu*, Kasîbhâradvâjas. vs. 1, Dh. 96, and *dakkhema*, Mahâsamayas. vs. 25; generally *eyyâma*.

In the second pl. we have only one instance of the shorter form *samâsetha* in the phrase *sabbhir eva samâsetha*; besides we have *eyyâtha* in *âgameyyâtha*, Cariy. i. 8, 5, *saṃvatteyyâtha*, Dh. 129, *pahiṇeyyâtha*, Dh. 215. In the third pl. we have always *eyyuṃ*=Skt. eyus.

The second sing. attanop. in *etho*, and the third in *etha*, are formed after the old fashion=Skt. ethâs, eta; the third is very frequent also in such verbs which otherwise follow the parassap. inflexion, as *rakkhetha*, Dh. v. 36, *abhittharetha*, v. 116, and in passives, as *jâyetha*, Dh. v. 58, from √jan. Besides, we have *âgaccheyyâtho*, *manasikareyyâtho* given by Alwis, Cat. 184, from Moggallâna's grammar. The first and second pers. pl. do not occur in any text, but the third is frequent, as *bhaveraṃ*, *gaccheraṃ*, &c.

Shortened forms of the regular opt. occur of some roots in *â*, as sthâ and dhâ: *adhiṭṭheyya* for *adhiṭṭhâyeyya*, Khudd. 16, *apanidheyya*, Pât. 16, and so we ought to read *parinibbeyaṃ* instead of *parinibbâyi*, Dîp. i. 24. From roots ending in *i* we have *niccheyya*, Dh. v. 256, for *nicchayeyya*, from nis+ci, *anabhineyya*, Pât. 4, *vineyya*, Khudd. 31, from nî; *jeyya* from ji, Dh. v. 103; from *i* we have *abbheyya*, Pât. 6, second *eyyâsi*, Jât. iii. 535. From *hû*=bhû: *huveyya* and *hupeyya* according to the Burmese writing, M. i. 6, 9; Trenckner, Pâli Misc. 62; besides, we have a contracted form *heyya*, only known from Rûpasiddhi ap. Alwis Introd. 48, but not yet found in any text.

The optatives of the seventh class can be shortened in two different ways; from *corayeyya* we get *coraye* on one side and *coreyya* on the other; from *bhâvayâmi* we have a contracted third sing. attanop. *bhâvetha*, Dh. v. 87 for *bhâvayetha*.

Besides this regular form of the optative, which corresponds to the optative of the Skt. first principal conjugation (comprising the first, fourth, sixth, and tenth classes), we have a few rests of the optative of the second principal conjugation.

Some of the roots ending in *â* can form, besides the regular optatives of the type *dadeyya* and *deyya* given above, the old *dajjâ*=Skt. dadyât, Dh. v. 224; first pers. *dajjaṃ*, Mah. 63, *dajjâhaṃ*, M. iii. 8, 1, and *dajjâmi*, Mah. 8. From this optative *dajjâ* was formed the verbal base *dajjati* (see above, p. 103) and this can again take the terminations of the optative, as in *dajjeyya*, Kacc. 256, *anuppadajjeyya*, Pât. 11; first pl. *anuppadajjeyyâma*, Pât. 11.

From jñâ we have *jâniyâ*, corresponding to Skt. jânîyât with shortening of the *î*, and contracted from this *jaññâ;* besides a form after the analogy of the verbs with vowel *a*, as *jâneyya.*

From *as*, 'to be,' we have an old optative which preserves throughout the *a* of the root dropped in Skt.:—

assaṃ	*assâma*
assa	*assatha*
assa, *siyâ*	*assu*, *siyuṃ*

The first pers. *assaṃ* occurs Dh. 186, the second *assa*, Jât. iii. 515, in the third both forms are equally frequent; *assâma* is found in Saccavibhanga, *assu*, Dh. v. 74, Jât. ii. 425.

From vad, 'to speak,' we have a second sing. *vajjâsi*, Jât. ii. 443; third pl. *vajju*, Jât. ii. 322, explained by the regular forms *vadeyyâsi* and *vadeyyuṃ*. By false analogy of this optative we have a present *vajjâmi* (just like *dajjâmi*, from *dajjaṃ*), *vajjemi* and a secondary optative *vajjeyya* given by Kacc. vi. 4, 19.

Kar forms its opt. in the parassap. third pers. sing. *kare* and *kareyya*, Dh. v. 43, Kacc. 263, pl. *kareyyâtha*, Dh. 147, *kareyyuṃ*, Dh. 187; attanop. *kubbetha*, C. vii. 4, 8. Besides, we have an old opt. *kayirâ* or *kayira* from karyât instead of kuryât, attan. *kayirâtha* or *kayiratha.*

Âp forms the old opt. *pappuyya* = prâpnuyât, Das. 37, C. vi. 4, 4.

Imperfect and Aorist.

First formation.

Parassapada.		Attanopada.	
aṃ a	*amha*	...	*amhase*
a o	*attha, û*	*ase*	*avhaṃ*
â a	*uṃ*	*attha*	*atthuṃ*

Second formation.

Parassapada.		Attanopada.	
iṃ	*imha*	...	*imhe*
i	*ittha*	*ise, ittho*	*ivhaṃ*
i	*iṃsu, isuṃ*	*ittha*	

The first form belongs to the imperfect and simple or strong aorist, which cannot be distinguished in Pâli, the second to the weak aorist, which is formed by adding the root *as*, 'to be,' as in Greek.

A third formation is only distinguished from the second by the plus of an *s*, so that we have *siṃ* instead of *iṃ*, &c. It is used mostly in verbs ending in vowels, and in causatives.

Examples of the first sing. in *aṃ* :—*avacaṃ*, Dh. 242, *addaṃ* and *addasaṃ*, 'I saw,' Jât. iii. 380, Anecd. 35, once with the present termination *addusâmi*, Oldenberg, K. Z. xxv. 320, *addasa*, M. ix. 1, 5, where the reading of the MSS. ought not to be changed; from dâ we have *adaṃ*, Jât. iii. 411, Cariy. i. 9, 30; from bhû *ahuṃ*, Jât. iii. 411; from çru, *assuṃ*, Jât. iii. 542.

Second pers. in *o* = as : *pamâdo*, Dh. v. 371; *âsado*, Jât. i. 414, iii. 207, C. vii. 3, 12; in *a*: *avaca*, Pât. 99; and from a reduplicated aorist identical in its formation to the Skt. avocaṃ : *avoca*, Dh. 185, *voca*, Dh. v. 133.

In the third pers. we have *â* and *a* = at: *abhavâ*, *ahuvâ*, Buddha 443, *addasa*, *udacchidâ*, Anecd. 77, and with a curious doubling of the *d*, unexplained as yet, *acchidda*, Dh. v. 351; *amarâ*, Jât. iii. 389 (v. l. *amarî*), 'he died.' *Ajjhagamâ*, Ras. 78, *papato*, C. v. 20, 5, is the only instance known of *o* in the third.

In the first pers. pl. we have *amha* or *mha* in *adamha*, Jât. ii. 71; *assumha*, Jât. ii. 400; *vuṭṭhamha*, Dîp. 79; *ahumha*, Dh. 105; besides a form corresponding to the Skt. *addasâma*, Dh. 96.

Second pers.: *ahuvattha*, Dh. 105; *avacuttha*, Pât. 5; *dattha*, Jât. ii. 181.

In the third pers. we have *û*, *u* and *uṃ*, all representing the Skt. us. Examples in *uṃ* are very numerous; *û* we have in *ajjhagû* from *adhigacchati*, Jât. i. 256, *anvagû*, Das. 36; and *u* in *âgu*, passim in Mahâsamayasutta. The following instances deserve notice because they form their aorist in Skt. with s: *aggahuṃ*, Mah. 253, *upaṭṭhahuṃ*, Mah. 132, 256, *randhayuṃ* Dh. v. 248, *abhikkâmuṃ*, Mahâsamayasutta vi. 4; *adakkhuṃ*, ib. vs. 3 corresponds to adrâkshus.

The second and third sing. of the attan. in *ase*, *attha*, are influenced by the corresponding forms of the *s* aorist in *ise ittha* (see later on). Examples are *suyattha*, Dh. 86, *adattha*, Jât. ii. 166. Besides, we have the regular form in *tha*=Skt. ta for inst. *avocatha*, Mah. 132, *adassatha*, Mah. 199, *khîyatha* Cariy. iii. 10, 1, passive *ajâyatha*, Mah. 24.

Mhase is also influenced by the *s* aorist, and besides it is a present termination; instances are *ahuvamhase*, *akaramhase*, F. Jât. 13, 38; *vaṇimhase*, Jât. ii. 137; *nimimhase*, Dh. 417; Jât. ii. 369; the form of the imperfect *mhasa* occurs in *akaramhasa*, Dh. 147. The second pl. in *vhaṃ* corresponds to the Skt. dhvaṃ, the third in *atthuṃ* is formed by false analogy from the sing. *attha.* Of these I have not found any instance in texts.

Brû forms *abravi* and *abruvi*, pl. *abravuṃ* and *abruvuṃ*.

From gâ we have a second pers. sing. *âgâ*, Fausb. S. N. 161, corresponding to Skt. agâs, a third *accagâ*, *upaccagâ* and *ajjhagâ*, Dh., corresponding to agât. From sthâ a third person *aṭṭhâ*, Mah. 78.

From kar we have the regular forms, and besides an abridged aorist *akâ*, Mah. 23, 37, corresponding to the vedic akar. Other forms of the same root will be given later on.

Labh forms an aorist *alatthaṃ*, Jât. i. 141; second pers. *alattha* or *lattha*, Dh. 240; third *alattha* = alabdha (attau). The first and second pers. are formed after the analogy of the third.

The first sing. of the second formation is contracted from the Skt. isham, as in vedic îm; examples are *abhâṇiṃ*, Jât. iii. 394, from *bhaṇ*, 'to speak,' *adassiṃ*, Cariy. i. 2, from darç, 'to see,' *udâtariṃ* from tar, Jât. ii. 317; *upâgamiṃ*, Jât. iii. 373; *ovâdiṃ*, Bv. xxvi. 4; we also have a form in *i* without the nasal *aggahi*, Jât. iii. 373; *upâgami*, Cariy. i. 195; *nimmini*, Cariy. ii. 6, 11; passive *ajâyi*, Cariy. iii. 5, 1. Sometimes we find *issaṃ* with a double instead of a single *s*, as in *sandhavissaṃ*, Dh. v. 153 (comp. Childers' Notes on Dhamm. 4, Trenckner, P. M. 56); *nandissaṃ*, Jât. 432, vs. 9, and most probably *titikkhissaṃ*, Dh. v. 320; some forms with a single *s* are given by Oldenberg, K. Z. xxv. 320; with change of *i* to *a* (Trenckner, p. 75), we have *icchasaṃ*, S. N. vii. 14, vs. 1, 6; *pamâdassaṃ*, M. N. 130; Ang. iii. 4, 6.

In the second pers. we have *i* or *î* in poetry when a long syllable is required, as in *âdiyi*, Suttavibh. i. 44; *kandî*, *gilî*,

Dh. v. 371; *agamî*, Mah. 6. In the third person we have the same termination in *âviñji*, Suttavibh. i. 127; *vedî*, Dh. v. 423; *abhinimmi* from *abhinimmâti*, Dh. 315; *akari* from kar, F. Jât. 13; or a new form in *isi*, as *agacchisi*, Mah. 206; *antaradhâyisi*, Mah. 112; *ajâyisi*, Mah. 18, 20.

In the first pers. pl. we have *imha* = ishma, as in *sarimha*, Dh. 188; *labhima*, Dh. 236; *apâyimha*, Jât. i. 360; in the second *ittha* = ishṭa, as in *saddhayittha*, Dh. 123; *dadittha*, Dh. 238; and in the third *iṃsu* or *isuṃ* = ishus.

In the attanopada the second pers. *ise* as given by the grammarians, is not found in any text (just like *ase* of the first formation); we find instead *ittho* = ishṭhâs in *atimaññittho*, Ten. Jât. 40; *asajjittho*, Jât. i. 297; *akkamittho*, Bv. ii. 53 (always spelt with the dental group).

In the third pers. we have *ittha* = ishṭa, as in *pasârayittha*, Jât. i. 135; *âsaṅkittha*, Jât. i. 151, and several passive forms given by Kacc. 289—293; comp. similar forms in the Mahâvastu, Senart's ed. p. 378.

In the first pers. pl. we have *imhe*; second, *ivhaṃ*; but these forms have not yet been found in any text. The third pl. terminates in *iṃsu*, *isuṃ*, or in *uṃ*, as *upagacchuṃ*, Mahâparin. 21 (see above, p. 113).

The first sing. of the third formation terminates in the *siṃ*, as *aññâsiṃ*, Pât. 95; *cintesiṃ*, Dh. 206; or *si*, as *cintesi*, Cariy. i. 8, 1; *adâsi*, Cariy. i. 9, 47; *paccaññâsi*, M. I. 6, 27, 28, where the reading of the MSS. should be followed.

Second pers. *si*, as *akâsi*, Suttavibh. i. 44, with assimilation *paṭivekkhi*, M. vi. 23, 8, and third the same as *adhosi*, Fausb. S. N. 150; *nimâsi*, Mah. 27; *avatthâsi*, Suttavibh. i. 79, from *avattharati*, *padhûpâsi*, M. I. 15, 4, Suttavibh. ii. 109, 132. *Udânesi*, Jât. i. 141; with assimilation *sakkhi*, Jât. iii. 424;

akkocchi, Dh. v. 4; *acchecchi*, Buddha, 441 (spelt wrongly *acchejji*, ib. 434); from kar, *akâsi* = akârshît; from har, *vihâsi*.

First pl. *siṃha* = sishma in *adâsiṃha*, Jat. iii. 120; second *sittha* = sishṭa.

The third pl. in *siṃsu* is not found, but is replaced by a form in *suṃ* or *ṃsu*, corresponding to Skt. sus, as in *adaṃsu*, *pâhesuṃ*, *âroccesuṃ*; from sthâ we have *aṭṭhaṃsu*, Dh. 233, and *uṭṭhiṃsu*, Mah. 166; from jñâ, *aññiṃsu*, Jât. iii. 303; from khyâ, *akkhaṃsu*, Jât. iii. 481; from vâ, *parinibbiṃsu*, Dîp. 51; from dhâ, *samâdahaṃsu*, Mahâsamayasutta vs. 2; from kar, *akaṃsu*.

After the false analogy of the aorists in *âsi* we find also some aorists of verbs ending in a consonant, as *agamâsi*, pl. *agamaṃsu* (not *agamaṃsuṃ*, which is a mistake of the Burmese MSS.); *addasâsuṃ*, Jât. ii. 256, and *adassaṃsu*, Papañca Sûdanî, ap. Alwis Introd. 73. Even the perfect *âha*, 'he spoke,' follows this inflexion, as we have *âhaṃsu*, Jât. i. 121, comp. âhaṃsus of the Mahâvastu ap. Minayeff, Pât. xliii. Another *âhaṃsu* is found in *payirudâhaṃsu*, 'they uttered,' from √har, comp. Weber, Hâla, 184; Ind. Streifen iii. 396.

The imperfect of the root *as*, 'to be,' is entirely formed after the analogy of these aorists:

âsiṃ âsi.	*âsiṃha.*
âsi.	*âsittha.*
âsi.	*âsiṃsu.*

The first pers. *âsi* occurs Cariy. i. 4, 1. For the third we find a form *ehi*, Bv. xvi. 7, which looks like an abbreviation of the fut. of *i*, *ehiti*, but perhaps the reading is incorrect.

Perfect.

Parassapada.		Attanopada.	
a.	*mha.*	*i.*	*mhe.*
e.	*ttha.*	*ttho.*	*vho.*
a.	*u.*	*ttha.*	*re.*

Verbs ending in consonants insert *i* between the root and the consonatal terminations. Examples are not very frequent: *hâ*, 'to leave,' forms *jahâra*, with a euphonic *r*, Kacc. 243; *chid*, *ciccheda*, ib. 242; *budh*, *bubodha*, Att. 203; *suc*, *susoca*, Att. 212; *ah*, *âha*, third pl. *âhu*; *vid*, *vidu*, Mah. 141.

Future.

Parassapada.		Attanopada.	
ssâmi.	*ssâma.*	*ssaṃ.*	*ssamhe.*
ssasi.	*ssatha.*	*ssase.*	*ssavhe.*
ssati.	*ssanti.*	*ssate.*	*ssante* (*ssare*).

The termination *aṃ* of the first sing. attan. is only an abbreviation of *âmi* in parassap. and occurs frequently in old texts as *dassaṃ*, *bhokkhaṃ*, Das. 7, 29; *hessaṃ*, *pûrayissaṃ*, Ten Jât. 91. This form is identical with the first sing. aorist according to the second formation in *issaṃ*, as *sandhâvissaṃ*, and this is the reason why they have often been mistaken one for the other.

The future may be formed from the root or from the special base. If it is formed from the root the terminations may be added directly, or by the auxiliary vowel *i*.

(*a*) Futures formed from the root directly: *pacessati*, Dh. 9; *vicessati*, Kacc. 27, both from *ci*; *vijessati*, from *ji*, Dh. 9; *dakkhati*=drâkshyati, √darç, *sakkhiti* from çak; *lacchati* from labh Dh. 96=latsyati for lapsyati (comp. the aorist *alattha* for alabdha), *sambhossâma* from *bhû*, Mah. 28; *vacchâmi* from *vac* Khuddasikkhâ 17; *pavekkhati* from viç, Mah. 153; *checchaṃ* from *chid*, Jât. iii. 500 (*samucchissatha*, Gr. 254, is formed after the false analogy of the other futures in *issati*); from *i* we have *esaṃ*, Jât. iii. 535, and *upessaṃ*, Dhaniya S. Childers, s. v. *upeti*; from *han*, first pers. pl., *hañchema*, Jât. ii. 418, with an *e*, instead of *â*, that I cannot explain. Trenckner takes this and *dakkhema*, Mahâsamay, v. 25, as optatives of the fut., but this is without any analogy. *Âhañchi*, M. i. 6, 8, Trenckner, P. M. 74; *bhejjati*, Ang. i. 5, 7, is most probably a mistake for *bhecchati* (like *acchejji* for *acchecchi*, above, p. 116).

The future is sometimes used in the sense of an imperfect, as *dassâmi*, Cariy. i. 3, 4; *pariyesissâmi*, Cariy. i. 6, 5; *pavissâmi* for *pavisissâmi*, from viç, Cariy. i. 9, 56 (*pavissâmi* as future occurs Jât. ii. 68). Perhaps these are only aorists with primary terminations like *addasâmi* (above, p. 112).

(*b*) Futures formed from the root by the auxiliary vowel *i*: *âgamissaṃ*, Jât. ii. 284 (and *âgamicchati*, Dh. ix. 12, formed after the false analogy of *dicchati*, if it is not merely a blunder); *niggahissati*, Dh. 96; *saṃvasissare*, in a passage of the Apadâna, quoted in Oldenberg's Buddha, 419; *labhissati*, Dh. 121; *nahâyissati* from snâ; *parinibbâyissati*, Dh. 333, from parinirvâ and *parinibbissaṃ*, Bv. xxvi. 23, with loss of the root-vowel.

(*c*) Futures formed from the special base, mostly by the auxiliary vowel *i*: *jinissati* from *ji*, and *cinissati* from *ci*, Dh. 209; *âgacchissati*, Dh. 84; *passissati*, Dh. 88, 89; *pajahissati* Dh. 311; *pahinissati*, Dh. 84; *pâpunissati*, Dh. 101; *sunissâmi* from çru, Jât. i. 129; *paridadhassati*, Dh. 115.

With *e* in *paridahessati*, Dh. v. 9; *niggahessâmi*, Dh. v. 326 (see above, p. 101).

In the 2nd pers. sing., 3rd pers. sing. and pl. we find sometimes *i*, instead of *a*, most probably from the *y* assimilated in the consonantal group, as *sakkhiti* for *sakkhati*, Sadda Nîti *sakkhinti*, Dhaniya S.; *dakkhisi*, F. J. 23; *dakkhinti*, Mah. 83; M. i. 7, 10.

In some futures the sibilant has migrated into *h*, as *kâhâmi* for karshyâmi, from kar, Cariy. i. 5, 9, Jât. i. 214; *kâhati*, Jât. ii. 443 (besides *kassâma*, Mah. 12; *kassaṃ* in a modern text, I. O. C. 121); comp. kâhîti of the Mahâvastu Minayeff, 109; *vihâhisi* from vihar, Dh. 68 (besides *vihassati*, Aruṇavatisutta, v. 2); *hâhasi*, from hâ, Jât. iii. 172; *paññâyihinti*, Jât. xvi. 1, 5, from prajñâ, *ehiti* from *i*. From *hû*=bhû we have *hohiti*= bhoshyati and *hehiti*=bhavishyati which may be further contracted into *heti*.

A peculiarity of the Pâli is the double future formed from bases like *dakkh* by the ordinary termination *issati*. The base *dakkh* came to be used exactly like a present base as we see from the imperf. *dakkiṃ*, Jât. i. 25 (which cannot be identified directly with the Skt. aorist adrâkshaṃ); from the present *dakkhati*, frequent in later texts, from the inf. *dakkhituṃ*, M. v. 1, 2; *dakkhitâye* (not *dakkhitâya*), Mahâsamayas, vs. 1, and from the causative *dakkhâpita*, Mil. 119. So we get a secondary future *dakkhissati*, *sakkhissati*, Dh. 84; *sukkhissati*, from çush, 'to dry,' Dh. 234; *pavakkhissaṃ* from vac, Cariy. i. 1, 2, *hehissati*, Kacc. 249.

A curious form is *dicchati*, Jât. 450, vs. 7 (*dicchati*, 'to see,' Alwis, Introd. 42, evidently derives from dṛiç). Trenckner, P. M. 61, following Vanaratana derives it from adikshat, but the comm. explains it by *dadanti*. I think it is the desiderative of *dâ* used as a new root with the meaning of the primitive verb, and this would speak in favour of Weber's explanation of *dakkhati* and *dekkhati* as desideratives (see Kuhn's Beitr. vii.

485 ff., Indische Streifen xiv. 69 ff.). Childers and Pischel (Beitr. vii. 450 ff.) explain them as futures, P. and S. Goldschmidt derive them from the part. dṛishṭa with a change of sounds similar to that in *dukkha*=duḥstha (see above, p. 39). The secondary base *sukkh* from çush (see the Causatives) speaks in favour of Goldschmidt's theory. As for *pavecchati*, Jât. i. 28, Mil. 375, I am unable to decide whether it is really the future of viç or, as Trenckner suggests, identical with *payacchati*.

Conditional.

Parassapada.		Attanopada.	
ssaṃ,	*ssamhâ.*	*ssaṃ*,	*ssamhase*
sse, ssa, ssasi,	*ssatha.*	*ssase*,	*ssavhe.*
ssâ, ssa, ssati,	*ssaṃsu.*	*ssatha*,	*ssiṃsu.*

With regard to the base the same rules apply to the conditional as to the future. Instances are, 1st pers. *apapessaṃ*, Jât. ii. 11 (v. l. *pâpeyyuṃ*); 2nd pers., *bhavissa* ib., *agghâpessasi*, Jât. ii. 31, v. l., for *agghâpeyyâsi*; 3rd pers., *agamissâ*, Kacc. 263; *alabhissa, asakkhissa*, Dh. 292; *paññâpessa*, and *abhavissati* in a passage of Saṃyuttaka Nikâya Buddha, 443, where Oldenberg wants to change it into *abhavissa*. For the pl. I can adduce no instances from texts.

Passive.

The passive is formed by adding the syllable *ya* already mentioned as characteristic of the third class. This syllable may be added to the root or to the present base, as *gacchîyati*, Kacc. 236; and *gamîyati*, Dîp. 70, from *gam*, 'to go; *vussati* and *vasîyati* from *vas*, 'to dwell;' *hâyati*, Dh. v. 364, and *hîyati*, Kacc. 257, from *hâ*, 'to forsake;' *gayhati* and *gheppati* from *grah*, 'to take;' *tâyati* from *tan*, 'to stretch,' Jât. iii. 283; Rûp. 37. About *vuḍḍhate* from *vah*, Kacc. 237 (see above, p. 51).

The rules about the assimilation of *y*, which is optional, are given above, p. 48 ff.

The terminations of the passive are those of the attanopada and parassapada without any fixed rule.

An anomalous form of the passive is *sussute*, from çru, 'to hear,' Indische Streifen, iii. 398.

Causative.

Just as *ya* is the characteristic of the passive, *aya* is the characteristic of the causative (being the seventh class). The root is generally strengthened before this termination, as *lâveti* from *lû*, 'to reap,' *nâyeti* from *nî*, to lead,' *gûhayati* from *guh*, 'to hide,' but we have also exceptions to this rule, as *cudita* instead of *codita*, M. iv. 16; *bhaṇeti* = bhâṇayati, *gameti* = gâmayati.

The second form of the causative with *p* is much more frequent in Pâli than in Skt. It may be formed almost from every root. Thus we have *jîrâpeti* from jar, Jât. i. 238; *bhiṃsâpeti* (v. l. *hiṃsâpeti*), from *bhî*, Pât. 15; *piṃsâpeti* from pish, Mah. 175, besides *piṃseti*, Jât. ii. 363; *jinâpeti* from *ji* (present base *jin*), Kaccâyanabhedaṭîkâ, I. O. C., 91; *sukkhâpeti*, Dh. 188, from çush (secondary base *sukkh*, derived from the Part. çushka, in *sukkhamâna*, Jat. i. 304); *upalâpeti* from *upalî*, M. v. 2, 21; Jât. ii. 266, comp. Rhys David's Buddhist Suttas, p. 5; *suṇâpeti*, Dh. 166, from çru (present base *suṇ*); *cetâpeti* from *ci* (through confusion with *cit*); *chejjapeti* from *chid*, Mil. 90; *ânâpeti* from *ânî*. On the difference in the signification of the two forms of the causative comp. Oldenberg KZ. xxv. 323.

A causative with double *p* is *viññâpâpeti*, from vijñâ, 'to cause to be asked for,' Pât. 105.

Pivati forms its caus. *pâyati* and *pâyeti*, *gah* : *gâheti* and *gâhâpeti* ; *han* : *haneti* and *ghâteti* ; *sampiyâyamâna*, Jat. i. 297, 361, ought to be corrected into *sampiyamâna*, according to Senart Mahâvastu, 556.

Desiderative.

The desiderative is formed from the reduplicated root, by adding an *s* : *jighacchati* from *ghas*, 'to eat,' sometimes written *jigacchati* (Grünwedel das sechste Kapitel d. Rûpasiddhi, p. 70) ; *jigucchati* from *gup* ; *titikkhati* from *tij* ; *cikicchati* and *tikicchati* from *kit* ; *pipâsati* and *pivâsati* from *pâ* ; *bubhukkhati* from *bhuj* ; *sussusati* from çru ; *dicchati* from *dâ* (see above) ; *jigiṃsati* from *har*. *Han* has a desiderative without reduplication, *pahaṃsati*, Jat. ii. 104 ; Pass. *pahaṃsiyati*, Mil. 326 ; *vîmaṃsati* from *man*, is only a phonetical change for *mîmaṃsati*.

Intensive.

Intensives are also formed from the reduplicated root, and sometimes take *ya*, as *daddallati* = jâjvalyate ; *lâlapatti* from lap ; *kâkucchati* from kath, Jât. i. 61, 160, 318, Mil. 85 ; without *ya*, but with a nasal in the reduplication syllable, we have *caṅkamati* from kram ; *jaṅgamati* from *gam*, *cañcalati* from *cal*.

Sâkacchati, 'to talk,' Pât. xv. seems to be formed after the false analogy of *kâkacchati* without reduplication.

Denominative.

Denominatives may be formed with and without reduplication. The terminations are the following :

(1) *Âyati* in *pabbatâyati*, *samuddâyati*, *ciccitâyati* and *ciṭiciṭâ-*

yati, 'to splash,' M. vi. 27, 7, Mil. 258; *dolâyati*, Jat. ii. 385; *tintiṇâyati*, Jat. i. 243, 244; *gaggarâyati*, Mil. 3; *verâyati*, Dîp. 83; *gaḷagaḷâyati*, Mahâparin, 48; *pariyâyati*, Samanta Pâsâd. 332; *pattiyâyati*, 'to believe,' Jât. i. 426, where Fausb. wrongly has adopted the reading *saddhiṃ yâyasi*, comp. Trenckner, P. M. 79; *harâyati*, M. i. 63, 1; Suttavibh. i. 68.

(2) *Iyati, îyati* in the examples given by Kacc. 233, which I have not found in any text, and besides in *paṭiseniyati*, Fausb. S. N. 64; *gaṇiyati*, Mil. 114; *aṭṭiyati*, 'to be hurt,' M. i. 63, 1.

(3) *Ayati, eti*, in the examples given by Kacc. 235, which are not found in any text, and besides in *bâheti* from bahis, 'to remove,' Senart Mahâvastu, 431; *yanteti*, Jât. i. 418; *vijaṭeti* and *vijaṭâpeti*, 'to disentangle;' *samodhâneti*, 'to join,' part. *samodhânita*, Jât. iii. 272; *theneti*, 'to steal,' Dh. 114, Jat. iii. 18.

For *sammanneti*, Ras. 69, we ought most probably to read *sammanteti* (Dh. 333), which is a denominative from mantra.

(4) *ati* in *pariyosânati*, 'to cease,' Dh. 331; *sârajjati*, 'to be ashamed,' Pât. xliv.; *osaṇhati*, 'to smooth,' C. v. 2, 3.

§ 19. Participles.

The present participle terminates in *ant* or *anta*, which is added to the present stem, e.g., *labhaṃ* or *labhanto*. About the declension of these participles and some other peculiarities, comp. p. 80. The same termination *ant* or *anta* is also used for the participle of the future, which, however, does not occur very frequently, e.g., *karissaṃ*, Dâṭh. iii. 80.

In the attanopada we have the terminations *mâna* and *âna* used almost without any difference from verbs of all classes, the latter being more or less restricted to the ancient language. From *kar* we have the regular form *kubbâna*=kurvâṇa, Dh. v. 217, but also *karâṇa* in *purekkharâṇa*, Fausb. S. N. 173; *kurumâna*, Sam. Pâs., 323, and *karamâna*; from çî, 'to lie down,' we have *sayamâna*, Kh. 16; from çush, 'to dry,' *sukkhamâna*, Jât. i. 304; from *vas*, 'to dwell,' *vussamâna*, Mah. 121; from *as*, 'to be,' *samâna*, Kacc. 258. A contraction takes place in *sampajâno* for *sampajânâno* from jñâ, 'to know,' Dh. v. 293.

The old perfect participle in vaṃs has almost totally disappeared; a few remaining traces have been given above, p. 80.

The past participle passive is formed by adding the terminations *ta* and *na* as in Saṃskṛit. These may be added to the root or to the present stem with or without the vowel *i*. From *vas* we have, according to Kacc. 291, *vusita* and *vuṭṭha*, e. g., *upavuṭṭha*, Cariy. ii. 3, 2; *parivuttha*, Pât. 6; *pavuttha*, Mil. 205; *vusitaṃ brahmacariyaṃ*, 'the religious duties have been fulfilled,' a locution very frequent in canonical texts, e. g., M. v. 1, 18; besides *vasita*, Mah. 123, where we ought to read *pabbajjâvasitaṭṭhâne* and *adhivattha*, Dh. 165, 341, 392 (*adhivuttha*, Mahâparin. 23). From *jhash*, 'to hurt,' we have *jhatta*, Mah. 146, Dh. 325, where the correct reading is *châtakajjhattâ*. From *pat*, 'to fall,' we have *patita* but also *patta* in *pattakkhandha*, 'crestfallen,' Mil. 5, Ass. S. 17. From *icchati*, 'to wish,' we have *iṭṭha* (or *yiṭṭha* after a word ending with a vowel) and *icchita*, which is wrongly given as a separate article by Childers. *Dhâ* forms the regular participle *hita*; *dhâta*, Mil. 238, Gr. 301, M. vi. 25, 1, S. ii. 51, is most probably from dhrâ (see M. 384). Somewhat irregular is *khata* for *khâta* from *khan*, 'to dig,' Kacc. 296, and the participles with *n*, where the Skt. drops it as *bandha*=baddha, Kacc. 130; *pilandha*, Mil. 337, from *pi+nah*; *randha*=raddha, Mil. 107; *parikanta*=parikṛitta, Suttavibh. i. 89 (but *parikatta*, Mil. 188).

Participles in *na* are somewhat more frequent in Pâli than in Skt. and in a few instances we find both forms from the same root, e. g., from *dâ* we generally have *dinna*, but also *datta* in *atta*=âdatta, Fausb. S. N. 150, 153, Dh. v. 406; from *rud*, 'to weep,' we have *rodita*, Ab. 165 and *ruṇṇa* or *roṇṇa*, Kh. 12, Das. 36, Jât. iii. 166, which is not an equivalent of *rudana* as Childers thought. From *lî* we have *sallîna*, 'depressed,' but also *sallita*, Cariy. iii. 11, 10. Jyâ forms *jîna*, Suttavibhanga, i. 220, comp. Pâṇ. viii. 2, 44, schol.; çâ, *sîna* in *saṃsînapatta*, S. N. 7. At v. 30 of the same Khaggavisâṇasutta we have *saṃchinna*, for which Senart Mahâvastu, 629, 630, gives the better reading *saṃchaṇṇa* from chard.

From this past participle passive is formed a secondary derivative by adding the suffixes *vat* or *vin* (the latter with lengthening of the *a*). This derivative has succeeded in its use to the lost past participle active in vaṃs. Examples are *vusitavanto*, Mil. 104; *hutavâ*, *hutâvî*, *bhuttavâ*, *bhuttâvî*, Kacc. 281.

The participle of necessity is formed by adding the terminations *tabba*, *tayya*=tavya, *anîya*, *ya*. These terminations can be joined with or without the vowel *i*. Examples with *tabba* are frequent enough: *jinitabba*, Dh. 101; *metabba*, Kamm. 8; *parijânitabba*, Dh. 151; *pativijjhitabba*, Dh. 2?9; *pariyâpuṇitabba*, Alw. N. 23; *tuṭṭhabba*, Jât. i. 476 – *tayya* is, as far as I know, only given by grammarians. *Anîya* we have in *karaṇîya*; *ya* in *sakkuṇeyya*, Mab. 141, and in *asaṃhîra* for asaṃharya, Dîp. 31.

Infinitive.

The infinitive generally terminates in *tuṃ*, as *gantuṃ*, 'to go;' *suṇituṃ*, 'to hear,' from the present stem, Mil. 91; *saṭṭhuṃ*, Ten Jât. 104; *thutuṃ*, from stu, 'to praise,' S. N. 38; *puṭṭhuṃ* =prashṭuṃ, 'to ask,' Parâbhavasutta, v. 1; *parimetum* from *mâ*, Mil. 192; *jinituṃ* from *ji*, Kacc. 319; *nikhâtuṃ*, from *khan*, Cariy. iii. 6, 16; from *budh* we have *patisambuddhuṃ* and *suboddhuṃ*, Kacc. 8. Besides we have also the ancient vedic terminations *tave*, *tuye*, and *tâye*, e. g., *pahâtave*, Dh. v. 34; *niketave*, Jât. iii. 274; *nidhetave*, Jât. iii. 17; *netave*, Dh. v. 180; with *tuye*, *gaṇetuye*, Bv. iv. 28; *marituye*, Therîgâthâ, 165; with *tâye*, *dakkhitâye*, Mahâsamayasutta v. 1; *jagghitâye*, Jât. iii. 226.

A curious form of the infinitive is *etase* from *i*, Therîgâthâ, 151.

Gerund.

The gerund is formed by adding the suffixes *tvâ* (*tvâna* and *tûna*) and *ya*. In Dhp. the use of *ya* is restricted to compound verbs as in Skt., but later on it is also used for the single verb. Before these terminations the root generally appears in the same shape as in the infinitive. Examples are very frequent: *tvâ* in *netvâ*=nîtvâ (inf. *netuṃ*); *chetvâ*=chittvâ (inf. *chettuṃ*); *bhutvâ*=bhuktvâ, Jât. iii. 53; *gantvâ*=gatvâ (inf. *gantuṃ*); *jetvâ*=jitvâ (inf. *jetuṃ*). From dṛç we have the anomalous gerund *disvâ*, where the *t* is entirely lost; *dassitvâ*, Suttavibhanga, ii. 64, should be changed into *passitvâ*. From *hâ*, 'to forsake,' we have the reduplicated form *jahetvâ*, Dîp. 56, and *jahitvâ*, Dhp. 85, 333; from sthâ, *uttiṭṭhitvâ*, Dh. 335; *upatiṭ-*

ṭhitvâ, Mil. 231. A contracted form is *anuvicca*=anuviditvâ (comm. *jânitvâ*), Jât. i. 459, Ang. ii. 2, 7, Fausb. S. N. xi.

Tvâna in *passitvâna*, Mah. 165; *jahitvâna*, Dh. 215; *suṇitvâna*, Das. Jât. 33; *jinitvâna*, Dh. 286; *chetvâna*, Dîp. 96; *vatvâna*, Dh. 193; *daditvâna*, Cariy. i. 9, 26; *pavakkhitvâna*, Mahâsamayasutta, 3. From the Skt. we can compare pîtvânaṃ, Pâṇ. vii. 1, 48.

Tûna in *kâtûna* or *kattûna*, Kacc. 310; Suttavibhanga, i. 96; *âpucchitûna*, Therîgâthâ, 165; *chaḍḍûna*, ib. 169; *nikkhamitûna*, Theragâthâ, 11; *sotûnaṃ*, at the beginning of the Mahâvagga of the Dîghanikâya I. O. C. 69.

Ya in *âhacca*=âhṛitya (Skt. âhârya), in *âhaccapâda*, 'a sort of bed,' frequent in the Vinaya; *âhacca*=âhatya from *han*, Mah. 45, Kacc. 302; *upahacca*=upahatya, ib., *uhacca*, Mahâsamayasutta, v. 3; *abbuyha* from â+bṛih, Dh. 255; *nikacca*=nikṛitya, Suttavibhanga, i. 90; and most probably also *paṭigacca* =pratikṛitya, with softening of the *k*, comp. Trenckner, Mil. 421; *paticca*=pratîtya, but *adhicca* I prefer to derive with Childers from adhṛitya, answering to Skt. adhârya. *Cicca*, Khuddasikkhâ and *sañcicca*, Pât. 3, 66, Suttavibhanga, i. 73, most probably stand for cintya=cintayitvâ (comm. *jânanto*). From *i* we have *anvâya*, frequent in Dh. formed after the false analogy of *mâya* from *mi*; from grah, *samuggahâya*, 'having embraced,' Fausb. S. N. 152.

Sometimes the termination *ya* of the gerund is dropped and the root alone remains, e. g., *abhiññâ* for *abhiññâya*, 'having known;' *paṭisaṅkhâ* for *paṭisaṅkhâya*, 'having reflected,' *anupâdâ* for *anupâdâya*, Dîp. 15.

In a few cases we find a gerund with double suffix combined from *ya* and *tvâ*, e. g., *abhiruyhitvâ* for *abhiruyha*, Kacc. 129;

ogayhitvâ for *ogayha*, Mah. 261; *sajjhitvâ* from *sad*, Bâlâvatâra, s. 58.

The suffix *tuṃ* of the inf. can be used also for the gerund, but this use seems to be limited to a few verbs. In the Pâṭimokkha we have a gerund, *abhihaṭṭhuṃ* from *har*, which agrees exactly with the corresponding Jaina forms puraükâuṃ and gantuṃ (see my Beiträge zur Gramm. d. Jaina Prâkṛit, p. 61). From Rhys David's and Oldenberg's note, Vinaya Texts, ii. 400, it appears as if they wanted to identify this form with those in *tvâna* and *tûna* like *nikkhamitûna;* we learn, however, from Hem. ii. 146, that in *abhihaṭṭhuṃ* and the corresponding Prâkṛit forms, the suffix of the inf. is used instead of the gerund. A similar form, distinguished only by the loss of the anusvâra is *daṭṭhu*=drashṭuṃ, 'having seen,' parallel with *disvâ*, S. N. 73, Theragâthâ, 48. The corresponding Prâk. form is given as daṭṭhuṃ by Hem. l. l.; but we have also in Jaina Prâk. forms without anusvâra, as kaṭṭu and haṭṭu from kar and har.

As an exercise for the student, I give the text of a Jâtaka, with a literal translation, and complete analysis of the words:—

VALÂHASSAJÂTAKA.

(*Fausböll's edition*, vol. ii., p. 127, ff.)

Atîte Tambapaṇṇidîpe Sirîsavatthun nâma yakkhanagaraṃ ahosi. Tattha yakkhiniyo vasiṃsu. Tâ bhinnanâvânaṃ âgatakâle alaṃkatapaṭiyattâ khâdaniyaṃ bhojaniyaṃ gâhâpetvâ dâsigaṇaparivutâ dârake aṃkenâdâya vâṇije upasaṃkamanti. Tesaṃ manussavâsaṃ âgat' amhâ 'ti sañjânanatthaṃ tattha tattha kasigorakkhâdîni karonte manusse gogaṇe sunakhe ti evam âdîni dassenti vâṇijânaṃ santikaṃ gantvâ "imaṃ yâguṃ pivatha bhattaṃ bhuñjatha khâdaniyaṃ khâdathâ" ti vadanti. Vâṇijâ ajânantâ tâhi dinnaṃ paribhuñjanti. Atha tesaṃ khâditvâ bhuñjitvâ vissamitakâle paṭisanthâraṃ karonti. "Tumhe katthavâsikâ kuto âgatâ kahaṃ gacchissatha kena kammena idhâgat' atthâ 'ti pucchanti "bhinnanâvâ hutvâ idhâgat' amhâ" ti vutte ca "sâdhu ayyâ amhâkam pi sâmikânaṃ nâvaṃ abhirûhitvâ gatânaṃ tîni saṃvaccharâni atikkantâni te matâ bhavissanti, tumhe pi vâṇijâ yeva mayaṃ tumhâkaṃ pâdaparicârikâ bhavissâmâ" ti vatvâ vatvâ te vâṇije itthikuttabhâvavilâsehi palobhetvâ yakkhanagaraṃ netvâ sace paṭhamagahitâ manussâ atthi te devasaṃkhalikâya bandhitvâ kâraṇaghare pakkhipanti. Attano vasanaṭṭhâne bhinnanâvamanusse alabhantiyo pana parato Kalyâṇiṃ orata Nâgadîpaṃ ti evaṃ samuddatîraṃ anuvicaranti, ayaṃ tâsaṃ dhammatâ. Ath' ekadivasaṃ pañcasatâ bhinnanâvâ vâṇijâ tâsaṃ nagarasamîpe uttariṃsu. Tâ tesaṃ santikaṃ gantvâ palobhetvâ yakkhanagaraṃ ânetvâ paṭhamagahitamanusse devasaṃkhalikâya bandhitvâ kâraṇaghare pakkhipitvâ jeṭṭhakayakkhinî jeṭṭhakavâṇijaṃ sesâ sese ti tâ pañcasatâ yakkhiniyo te pañcasate vâṇije attano sâmike akaṃsu. Atha sâ jeṭṭhayakkhinî rattibhâge vâṇije niddaṃ gate uṭṭhâya gantvâ kâraṇaghare manusse mâretvâ maṃsaṃ khâditvâ âgacchati. Sesâpi tath' eva karonti. Jeṭṭhayakkhiniyâ manussamaṃsaṃ khâditvâ âgatakâle sarîraṃ sîtalaṃ hoti. Jeṭṭhavâṇijo parigaṇhanto tassâ yakkhinibhâvaṃ ñatvâ "imâ pañcasatâpi yakkhiniyo bhavissanti, amhehi palâyituṃ vaṭṭatîti" punadivase pâto va mukhadhovanatthâya gantvâ sesavâṇijânaṃ ârocesi: imâ yakkhiniyo na mânusiyo, aññesaṃ bhinnanâvânaṃ âgatakâle te sâmike katvâ amhe khâdissanti, etha amhe palâyâmâ" ti tesu aḍḍhateyyasatâ "mayaṃ etâ vijahituṃ na sakkhissâma, tumhe gacchatha, mayaṃ na palâyissâmâ" ti âhamsu. Jeṭṭhavâṇijo attano vacanakare aḍḍhateyyasate gahetvâ tâsaṃ bhîto palâyi. Tasmiṃ pana kâle Bodhisatto valâhassayoniyaṃ nibbatti, sabbaseto kâkasîso muñjakeso iddhimâ vehâsaṃgamo ahosi. So Himavantato âkâse uppatitvâ Tambapaṇṇidîpaṃ gantvâ tattha Tambapaṇṇisare pallale sayaṃjâtasâliṃ khâditvâ gacchati, evaṃ gacchanto va "janapadaṃ gantukâmâ atthi janapadaṃ gantukâmâ atthîti" tikkhattuṃ karuṇâya paribhâvitaṃ mânusivâcaṃ bhâsati. Te tassa vacanaṃ sutvâ upasaṃkamitvâ añjaliṃ paggayha "sâmi mayaṃ janapadaṃ gamissâmâ" ti âhaṃsu. "Tena hi mayhaṃ piṭṭhiṃ abhirûhathâ" ti. Ath' ekacce abhirûhiṃsu ekacce vâladhiṃ gaṇhimsu ekacce añjaliṃ paggahetvâ aṭṭhaṃsu yeva. Bodhisatto antamaso añjalim paggahetvâ ṭhite sabbe pi te aḍḍhateyyasate vâṇije attano ânubhâvena janapadaṃ netvâ sakasakaṭṭhânesu patiṭṭhâpetvâ attano vasanaṭṭhânaṃ agamâsi. Tâpi kho yakkhiniyo aññesaṃ âgatakâle te tattha ohînake aḍḍhateyyasate manusse vadhitvâ khâdiṃsu.

Translation.

In former times there was in the island of Lankâ a Yakkha city called Sirîsavatthu. Therein dwelt Yakkhinîs. These, whenever a shipwreck took place, in splendid clothing, taking soft and hard food, surrounded by female slaves, carrying children on their hips, went to meet the merchants. That they might think "We have come to an abode of men," they would show here and there men ploughing and tending cattle and so forth, herds of cattle, dogs, etc., and approaching the merchants they would say, "Drink this rice gruel, partake of this rice, eat this food." The merchants, unawares, enjoy what is given by them. Thus having eaten and enjoyed, while resting, they exchange friendly greetings. They ask: "Where do you live? whence do you come? whither are you going? on what business have you come hither?" They answer: "We have come hither, having been shipwrecked." [Then the Yakkhhinîs say]: "Well, sirs, three years have passed since our husbands went on board ship and went away; they must be dead; you are also merchants, we will be your servants." Thus they enticed those merchants with female blandishments, and leading them to the Yakkha city, the first men being captured, having bound them as it were with supernatural chains, they hurry them into the abode of destruction. If they do not obtain shipwrecked men near their own place of abode, they wander along the sea-shore as far as Kalyâṇi on the other side, and Nâgadîpa on this side, and this is their custom. On a certain day, 500 merchants came to their city. The females approaching them, enticed them, and bringing them to the Yakkha city, binding the men whom they first captured as with supernatural chains, they hurried them into the abode of destruction. The first Yakkhinî took the chief merchant, the others the remainder, and so the 500 Yakkhinîs made the 500 merchants their husbands. Then the chief Yakkhinî in the night time, when the merchants had gone to sleep, rising, goes to the abode of destruction, and, killing men, eats their flesh, and returns. The others do likewise. When the chief Yakkhinî returned, after having eaten the human flesh, her body was cold. The chief merchant, having embraced her, knew that she was a Yakkhinî, and thought: "These must be 500 Yakkhinîs; we must escape." On the morrow, in the early morning, on going to wash his mouth, he told the other merchants: "These are Yakkhinîs, not human beings; when other shipwrecked men come, they will make them their husbands, and devour us. Shall we not flee? But 250 said: "We are unable to leave them; you go; we shall not flee." The chief merchant, having persuaded the 250 by his advice, fled, terrified at the females. Now at that very time the Bodhisattva was born from the womb of a mare; he was pure white, black-headed, muñja-haired, possessed of supernatural power, being able to go through the air. Rising through the air from the Himavanta, he went to the isle of Tambapaṇṇi, and having eaten paddy, produced spontaneously in the lakes and ponds of Tambapaṇṇi, he went on, and thus proceeding, said compassionately three times in a well modulated human voice: "Does any person wish to go? Does any person wish to go? They, hearing the speech, came near with folded hands, and said: "Sir, we folk wish to go." "Then get upon my back," said he. Then some got on his back, some seized his tail, but some stood with folded hands. Bodhisatta, by his own supernatural power, conveying all the 250 merchants, even those standing with folded hands, placing each in his own place, returned to his own abode. But the Yakkhinîs, when the time of the others had come, killed the remaining 250, and ate them.

This story is another version of the well-known myth of the Sirens, as was pointed out for the first time by Dr. Morris, in the "Academy" of Aug. 27, 1881 (reprinted in the "Indian Antiquary" for October, 1881, pp. 292-3).

Atîte, 'in former times,' loc. sing. of the past part. of *i*, 'to go,' with *ati*.

Tambapaṇṇidîpe, 'in the island of Ceylon,'=Tâmraparṇidvîpe, loc. sing., tâmraparṇi literally means 'copper leaf,' most probably from the colour of the soil in the island. Ceylon was called the 'Island of the Demons,' as can be seen from Senart "La Légende du Bouddha," p. 272, et seq. Allusion is made to this myth also in the Lalitavistara, p. 196, ed. Calc.:

Laghu gagane vrajase kṛipajâto râkhasadvîpaṃ
Vyasanaçata manujân tada gṛhya kshame sthapesi.

Sirîsavatthun (v. l. °*vatthu*) nom. sing. of a neuter *u*-stem About the locality of this fabulous town nothing is known to me.

Nâma, nom. sing. of a neuter *n*-stem.

Yakkhanagaraṃ, nom. sing. of a neuter *a*-stem.

Ahosi, 3rd. pers. sing. Aorist of *bhû* or *hû*, 'to be.'

Tattha=tatra, 'there,' adverb of place.

Yakkhiniyo, nom. pl. of *yakkhinî*, 'a female *yakkha*.'

Vasiṃsu, 3rd. pl., aorist of *vas*, 'to dwell.'

Tâ, nom. pl. fem. of the demonstr. pronoun.

Bhinnanâvânaṃ, gen. pl. of a bahuvrîhi compound from *bhinna* and *nâvâ*, 'ship.' *Bhinna* is the past part. pass. of *bhid*, 'to break,' and the whole compound means 'shipwrecked.'

Âgatakâle. *Âgata* is past part. pass. from *â*+*gam*, 'to go,' and *kâle*, loc. of *kâla*, 'time.'

Alaṃkatapaṭiyattâ, a compound of two past participies. *Alaṃkata*=Skt. alaṃkrita, 'adorned, embellished,' from *alaṃ*+*kar*. *Paṭiyatta* from prati+yat, 'to prepare, to dress.' The whole compound stands in the nom. pl. f.

Khâdaniyaṃ, acc. sing. n. of the part. of necessity of √*khâd*, 'to eat.' It means literally, 'that can be chewed,' i.e., 'solid food.'

Bhojaniyaṃ, acc. sing. n. of the part. of necessity of √*bhuj*, 'to eat,' means, in opposition to *khâdaniyaṃ*, 'soft, or wet food,' as boiled rice, etc.

Gâhâpetvâ, gerund of the causative of √*gah*, 'to take,' lit. 'to cause to be taken.'

Dâsigaṇaparivuṭâ, nom. pl. f., parallel to *alaṃkatapaṭiyattâ*. *Dâsigaṇa*, 'a troop of female slaves,' *parivuṭa*, past part. pass. of *pari*+*var*, 'to surround.'

Dârake, acc. pl. of *dâraka*, 'child.'

Aṃkenâdâya. *Aṃkena*, instr. sing. of *aṃka*, 'hip,' *âdâya*, gerund of *â*+*dâ*, 'to take.' The whole means 'having taken on the hip.'

Vâṇije, acc. pl. of *vâṇija*, 'merchant.'

Upasaṃkamanti, iii. pl. pres. of upa+saṃ+kraṃ, 'to approach.'

Tesam, gen. pl. m. of the demonstr. pronoun.

Manussavâsaṃ, acc. sing. of *manussa*, 'man,' and *vâsa*, 'dwelling.'

Âgat' stands in sandhi for *âgatâ*, nom. pl. of the past part. of *â*+*gam* (see above, *âgatakale*).

Amhâ ti stands in sandhi for *amha iti*. *Amha* is 1st pers. pl. pres. of the verb subst. *as*. *Iti* is generally used after a quotation.

Sañjânanatthaṃ, composed from *sañjânana*, 'perceiving,' and the acc. of *attha*, 'purpose.' It means 'for the purpose of perceiving.'

Tattha, *tattha*, see above. The repetition is distributive, 'here and there.'

Kasigorakkhâdîni, *kasi*=kṛishi, 'ploughing,' *gorakkhâ*, 'cow-keeping;' *âdîni* is the neuter pl. of *âdi*, 'etc.' The whole compound is an acc. dependent from the following *karonte*.

Karonte, acc. pl. m. pres. part. of *kar*, 'to make.' This belongs to *manusse* and depends from *dassenti*.

Manusse, acc. pl. of *manussa*, 'man.'

Gogaṇe, acc. pl. 'herds of cattle.'

Sunakhe, acc. pl. of *sunakha*, 'dog.'

Ti=*iti*, see above.

Evaṃ, particle, 'thus.'

Ádîni, acc. pl. n. of *âdi*, 'etc.'

Dassenti, 3rd pers. pl. pres. caus. of darç, 'to see.'

Vâṇijânaṃ, gen. pl. of *vâṇija*, 'merchant,' dependent from *santikaṃ*.

Santikaṃ, acc. of *sa*+*antika*, 'near.'

Imaṃ, acc. sing. f. of the demonst. pronoun.

Yâguṃ, acc. sing. of *yâgu*=yavâgu, 'rice-gruel,' a fem. *u*-stem.

Pivatha, 2nd pers. pl. imp. of *pibati*, 'to drink.'

Bhattaṃ, acc. sing. of *bhatta*=bhakta, 'boiled rice.'

Bhuñjatha, 2nd pers. pl. imp. of *bhunjati*, 'to eat.'

Khâdaniyaṃ, see above.

Khâdatha, 2nd pers. pl. imp. of *khâdati*, 'to eat.' The long ā is the crasis, as in *amhâ*, above.

Vâṇijâ, nom. pl. of *vâṇija*.

Ajânantâ, nom. pl. of the pres. part. of jñâ, 'to know,' with *a* privativum, 'not knowing.'

Tâhi, instr. pl. f. of the demonstr. pronoun.

Dinnaṃ, acc. sing. past part. of *dâ*, 'to give.' The substantive is understood.

Atha, particle, 'then.'

Khâditvâ, gerund from *khâd*.

Bhuñjitvâ, gerund from *bhuj*.

Vissamitakâle, similar to *âgatakâle*, above. *Vissamita*, past part. from *vi*+çram, 'to rest.'

Paṭisanthâraṃ, acc. sing. of a masc. *a*-stem.

Karonti, 3rd pers. pl. pres. of *kar*.

Tumhe, nom. pl. pers. pronoun, 2nd pers.

Katthavâsikâ, nom. pl. of compound from *kattha*=kutra, 'where,' and *vâsika*, 'living.'

Kuto=kutas, 'whence.'

Âgatâ, nom. pl. of *âgata*, see above.

Kahaṃ, interrog. particle, 'where, whither.'

Gacchissatha, 2nd pers. pl. fut. of *gacch*, the present stem of *gam*, 'to go.'

Kena kammena, instr. sing. of the interrog. pronoun and *kamma*=karman, 'business.'

Idhâgat'=*idha*+*âgatâ*.

Attha, 2nd pers. pl. pres. of *as*, 'to be.'

Pucchanti, 3rd pers. pl. pres. of *pucch*, 'to ask.'

Bhinnanâvâ, nom. pl., see above.

Hutvâ, gerund of *bhû* or *hû*, 'to be.'

Vutte, locative absolute of the past part. of *vac*, 'to speak.'

Ca, 'and,' copulative particle.

Sâdhu, neuter adjective, 'well.'

Ayyâ, voc. pl. of ârya, 'sir.'

Amhâkaṃ, gen. pl. personal pronoun, 1st pers.

Pi=*api*, 'also.'

Sâmikânaṃ, gen. pl. of *sâmika*, 'husband.'

Nâvaṃ, acc. sing. of *nâvâ*, 'ship.'

Abhirûhitvâ, gerund of *abhiruh*, 'to mount.'

Gatânaṃ, gen. pl. of *gata*. This belongs to *sâmikânaṃ* and depends from *tîṇi saṃvaccharâni atikkantâni*.

Tîṇi, nom. pl. n. of the numeral stem *ti*, 'three.'

Saṃvaccharâni, nom. pl. of a neuter *a*-stem.

Atikkantâni, nom. pl. n. past part. of ati+kram, 'to go beyond, to pass.'

Te, nom. pl. m. demonstr. pronoun.

Matâ, nom. pl. past part. of *mar*, 'to die.'

Bhavissanti, 3rd pers. pl. fut. of *bhû*, 'to be.'

Tumhe, see above.

Yeva in Sandhi for *eva*.

Mayaṃ, nom. pl. pers. pronoun, 1st pers.

Tumhâkaṃ, gen. pl. pers. pronoun, 2nd pers., see above, *amhâkaṃ*.

Pâdaparicârikâ, nom. pl. f. from *pâda*, 'foot,' and *paricârika*, 'servant.'

Bhavissâma, 1st pers. pl. fut. of *bhû*.

Vatvâ, gerund from *vac*, 'to say.'

Itthikuttabhâvavilâsehi, compound from *itthi* = strî, 'woman,' *kutta* of unknown etymology, most probably synonymous with the following *vilâsa*, 'charm, beauty.' The whole stands in the instr. pl.

Palobhetvâ, gerund of the caus. of *pra* + *lubh*, 'to seduce.'

Yakkhanagaraṃ, the acc. to denote the direction, 'to the Yakkha city.'

Netvâ, gerund of *nî*, 'to lead.'

Sace, conjunction, 'if.'

Paṭhamagahitâ, from *paṭhama*, 'first,' and *gahita*=gṛihîta, past part. of grah, 'to take.' The whole stands in the nom. pl.

Atthi, 3rd pers. sing., instead of the plural.

Devasaṃkhalikâya, from *deva*, 'god,' and *saṃkhalikâ*=çṛiṅkhala, 'a chain.' The whole is a tappurisa compound, and stands in the instr. case.

Bandhitvâ, gerund from *bandh*, 'to bind.'

Kâraṇaghare, loc. of *kâraṇa*, 'destruction,' and *ghara*=gṛiha, 'house.'

Pakkhipanti, 3rd pers. pl. pres. of pra + kship, 'to throw.'

Attano, gen. sing. of *attâ*=âtman, 'self.'

Vasanaṭṭhâna, loc. of *vasana*, 'dwelling,' and sthâna, 'place.'

Alabhantiyo, nom. pl. f. of the pres. part. of *labh*, 'to obtain,' with a privativum.

Pana=punar, 'again.'

Parato and *orato*, abl. sing. of *para*, 'further,' and *ora*, 'hither.'

Kalyâṇim and Nâgadîpaṃ, acc. of direction. *Kalyâṇi* must be the modern Kaelani on the Kaelani Gaṅgâ, about six miles from Colombo, where there is a celebrated Buddhist temple. *Nâgadîpa* is most probably identical with the *Naggadîpa* of the Mahâvaṃsa (p. 46), which island Vijaya is said to have touched on his way from Bengal to Ceylon, but nothing can be made out about the situation of this island.

Samuddatîraṃ acc. from *samudda*, 'the sea,' and *tîra*, 'the shore.'

Anuvicaranti, 3rd pers. pl. pres. of *anu+vi+car*, 'to wander along.'

Ayaṃ, nom. sing. f. of the demonstr. pronoun.

Tâsaṃ, gen. pl. f. of the demonstr. pronoun *ta*.

Dhammatâ, 'occupation,' f. *â*-stem.

Ekadivasaṃ, from *eka*, 'one,' and *divasa*, 'day.' Acc. to denote time.

Pañcasatâ, nom. pl. of *pañca*, 'five,' and *sataṃ*, 'hundred.'

Nagarasamîpe, loc. of *nagara*, 'town,' and *samîpa*, 'neighbourhood.'

Uttariṃsu, 3rd pers. pl. aorist from *ut+tar*, 'to cross over.'

Gantvâ, gerund from *gam*, 'to go.'

Ânetvâ, see *netvâ*, above.

Pakkhipitvâ, gerund from pra+kship.

Jeṭṭhakayakkhinî, 'the chief or first Yakkhinî.'

Sesâ, nom. pl. f. and *sese*, acc. pl. m. of *sesa*, 'other.'

Vâṇije and *sâmike*, acc. pl.

Akaṃsu, 3rd pers. pl. aorist from *kar*.

Rattibhâge, loc. to denote time.

Niddaṃ, acc. of *niddâ*, 'sleep,' to denote the direction, dependent from *gate*.

Gate, acc. pl. belongs to *vâṇije*.

Uṭṭhâya, gerund from *ut*+sthâ, 'to get up.'

Mâretvâ, gerund of the caus. of *mar*, means 'to kill.'

Âgacchati, 3rd pers. sing. pres. of *â*+*gacch*.

Jeṭṭhakayakkhiniyâ, gen. sing. dependent from *sarîraṃ*.

Manussamaṃsaṃ, acc. 'human flesh.'

Sîtalaṃ, neuter adjective.

Sarîraṃ, nom. of a neuter *a*-stem.

Hoti, 3rd pers. sing. pres. of *bhû* or *hû*.

Pariganhanto, nom. sing. of a pres. participle, from pari+grah, 'to embrace.'

Tassâ, gen. sing. f. demonstr. pronoun.

Yakkhinibhâvaṃ, acc. 'quality of a Yakkhinî.'

Ñatvâ, gerund from jñâ, 'to know.'

Imâ, nom. pl. f. demonstr. pronoun.

Bhavissanti, 3rd pers. pl. fut. of *bhû*.

Amhehi, dat. pl. pers. pronoun, 1st pers.

Palâyituṃ, inf. of *palâyati*, 'to flee.'

Vaṭṭati, 3rd pers. sing. pres. of vart, 'it behoves, it is right.'

Punadivase, l. of *puna*, 'again,' and *divasa*, 'day,' means, 'on the next day.'

Pâto=prâtar, 'early.'

Va for *eva* with the initial *e* elided after a long vowel.

Mukhadhovanatthâya, compound of *mukha*, 'mouth,' *dhovana*, 'washing,' and *attha*, 'purpose,' the whole in the dat. to denote the intention.

Sesavâṇijânaṃ, gen. pl. used instead of the dat. dependent from *ârocesi*.

Ârocesi, 3rd pers. sing. aor. from *â+ruc*, 'to tell.'

Mânusiyo, nom. pl. of *mânusî*, the f. of *mânusa*, 'man.'

Aññesaṃ, gen. pl. m. of *añña*, formed according to the pronominal inflexion.

Amhe, acc. pl. m. of the pers. pronoun, 1st pers.

Khâdissanti, 3rd pers. pl. fut. of *khâd*.

Etha, 2nd pers. pl. imp. of *i*, 'to go.'

Amhe, nom. pl. m. of the pres. pronoun, 1st. pers.

Palâyâma, 1st. pers. pl. imp. of *palâyati*.

Tesu, loc. pl. m. demonstr. pronoun.

Aḍḍhateyyasatâ=ardhatṛitîyaçatâḥ, literally, 'the third hundred half,' a very common way of expressing the number 250.

Etâ, acc. pl. f. demonstr. pronoun.

Vijahituṃ, inf. of *vi+hâ*, 'to forsake.'

Sakkhissâma, 1st pers. pl. of çak, 'to be able,' with the double fut. suffix, see p. 119.

Tumhe, nom. pl. m. pers. pronoun, 2nd pers.

Gacchatha, 2nd pers. pl. imp. of *gam*, 'to go.'

Palâyissâma, 1st pers. pl. fut. of *palâyati*.

Âhaṃsu, 3rd pers. pl. aorist of *ah*, 'to say.'

Vacanakare, loc. sing. of *vacana+kara*.

Aḍḍhateyyasate, acc. pl.

Gahetvâ, gerund of grah, 'to take.'

Tâsaṃ, gen. pl. f. demonstr. prononn.

Bhîto, past part. of *bhî*, 'to fear.'

Palâyi, 3rd. pers. sing. aor.

Tasmiṃ, loc. sing. m. demonstr. pronoun.

Pana=punar, 'again.'

Bodhisatto, nom. sing.

Valâhassayoniyaṃ, compound from *valâha*, 'cloud,' *assa*, 'horse,' and *yoni*, 'womb.' The whole stands in the loc. sing.

Nibbatti, 3rd pers. aor. of *nis+vart*, 'to be born.'

Sabbaseto=sarvaçveta, 'all white.'

Kâkasîso, literally, 'crow-headed.'

Muñjakeso, 'with hair like the *muñja*,' a certain sort of grass.

Iddhimâ=ṛiddhimant, nom. sing. of a stem in *ant*.

Vehâsaṃgamo, nom. sing. of *vehâsa*=vihâyasa, 'the open air,' in the acc. case, and *gama*, verbal adjective of *gam*, 'to go.'

So, nom. sing. m. of the demonstr. pronoun.

Himavantato, abl. sing of *Himavanta*, 'the Himâlaya,' with suffix *to*.

Âkâse, loc. sing. of *âkâsa*, 'the sky.'

Uppatitvâ, gerund from *ud+pat*, 'to rise.'

Tambapaṇṇidîpaṃ, acc. of direction.

Sare and *pallale*, are loc. sing. of *sara*=saras, 'the pond,' and *pallala*,=palvala, 'the pool.'

Sayaṃjâtasâliṃ, acc. sing. of *sayaṃ*=svayam, 'self,' *jâta*, past part. from *jan*, 'to produce,' and *sâli*, 'rice.'

Janapadaṃ, acc. of direction. *Janapada* is a compound from *jana*, 'people,' and *pada*, 'place.'

Gantukâmâ, nom. pl. of *gantu*, inf. of *gam*, 'to go,' and *kâma*, 'wishing.'

Atthi stands for the plural. The whole sentence is a question.

Tikkhattuṃ=ṭrishkṛitvas, numeral adverb, 'three times.'

Karuṇâya, instr. sing. of *karuṇâ*, 'mercy,' a fem. *â*-stem.

Paribhâvitaṃ, acc. sing. f. of the past part. caus. of *pari*+*bhû*, 'to surround.'

Mânusivâcaṃ, acc. sing. of the f. of *mânusa*, 'human,' and *vâç*, 'speech.'

Bhâsati, 3rd pers. sing. pres. of bhâsh, 'to speak.'

Tassa, gen. sing. m. demonstr. pronoun.

Vacanaṃ, acc. sing. of a neuter *a*-stem.

Sutvâ, gerund of çru, 'to hear.'

Upasaṃkamitvâ, gerund of upa+saṃ+kram, 'to approach.'

Añjalim, acc. sing. of a m. *i*-stem.

Paggayha, gerund of pra+grah, 'to stretch forth.'

Sâmi, voc. sing.

Gamissâma, 1st. pers. pl. fut. of *gam*.

Mayhaṃ, dat. instead of gen. sing. of the pers. pronoun, 1st pers.

Piṭṭhiṃ, acc. of *piṭṭhî*=pṛishṭha, 'back.'

Abhirûhatha, 2nd pers. pl. imp. of *abhi*+*ruh*, 'to ascend.'

Ekacce, nom. pl. of *ekacca*=ekatya (see above, p. 49), formed according to the pronominal inflexion.

Abhirûhiṃsu, 3rd pers. pl. aorist of *abhi*+*ruh*.

Vâladhiṃ, acc. sing. of a m. *i*-stem.

Gaṇhiṃsu, 3rd pers. pl. aorist of grah.

Aṭṭhaṃsu, 3rd pers. pl. aorist of sthâ, 'to stand.'

Antamaso, abl. of the superlative *antama*, 'the last,' formed with the suffixças (see p. 68).

Ṭhite, acc. pl of *ṭhita*, past. part. of sthâ.

Anubhâvena, instr. sing. of a m. *a*-stem.

Sakasakaṭṭhânesu, compound from *saka*=svaka, 'own,' and *ṭhâna*, 'place.' The repetition of *saka* is distributive.

Patiṭṭhâpetvâ, gerund of the caus. of prati+sthâ, 'to establish.

Agamâsi, 3rd pers. sing. aorist of *gam*.

Tâpi=*tâ api*.

Kho=khalu, 'indeed.'

Aññesaṃ, gen. pl. m. of *añña*, according to the pronominal inflexion.

Ohînake, acc. pl. of the past part. of *ava*+*hâ*, 'to forsake,' with the secondary suffix *ka*.

Vadhitvâ, gerund of *vadh*, 'to kill.'

www.ingramcontent.com/pod-product-compliance
Lightning Source LLC
Chambersburg PA
CBHW021114020726
47500CB00003B/752
9783743393295